AQUARIUS 2002

Teri King's Astrological
Horoscopes for 2002

Aquarius

Teri King's complete horoscope
for all those whose birthdays fall
between 20 January and 18 February

Teri King

Thorsons

Thorsons
An Imprint of HarperCollins*Publishers*
77–85 Fulham Palace Road
Hammersmith, London W6 8JB

The Thorsons website address is: www.thorsons.com

Published by Thorsons 2001

1 3 5 7 9 10 8 6 4 2

Teri King asserts the moral right to be
identified as the author of this work

A catalogue record for this book
is available from the British Library

ISBN 0 00 712138 5

Printed and bound in Great Britain by
Omnia Books Limited, Glasgow

Contents

Aquarius
20 January to 18 February

Ruling Planet: **Uranus**
Element: **Air**
Quality: **Masculine**
Planetary Principle: **Truth**
Primal Desire: **To know and understand**
Colours: **All colours of the spectrum**
Jewel: **Opal**
Day: **Saturday**
Magical Number: **22**

Famous Aquarians
Paul Newman, Jack Lemmon, Charles Darwin,
Clark Gable, Galileo, Franklin D Roosevelt,
Jeanne Moreau, Abraham Lincoln, Virginia Woolf,
James Joyce, Norman Mailer, François Truffaut,
Thomas Edison

Introduction

Astrology has many uses, not least of these its ability to help us to understand both ourselves and other people. Unfortunately there are many misconceptions and confusions associated with it, such as that old chestnut – how can a zodiac forecast be accurate for all the millions of people born under one particular sign?

The answer to this is that all horoscopes published in newspapers, books and magazines are, of necessity, of a general nature. Unless an astrologer can work from the date, time and place of your birth, the reading given will only be true for the typical member of your sign.

For instance, let's take a person born on 9 August. This person is principally a subject of Leo, simply because the Sun occupied that section of the heavens known as Leo during 23 July to 22 August. However, when delving into astrology at its most serious, there are other influences which need to be taken into consideration – for example, the Moon. This planet enters a fresh sign every 48 hours. On the birth date in question it may have been in, say, Virgo. And if this were the case it would make our particular subject Leo (Sun representing willpower) and Virgo (Moon representing instincts) or, if you will, a Leo/Virgo. Then again the rising sign of 'ascendant' must also be taken into consideration. This also changes constantly as the Earth revolves: approximately every two hours a new section of the heavens comes into view – a new sign passes over the horizon. The rising sign is of the utmost importance, determining the image projected by the subject to the outside world – in effect, the personality.

The time of birth is essential when compiling a birth chart. Let us suppose that in this particular instance Leo was rising at the time of birth. Now, because two of the three main influences are Leo, our sample case would be fairly typical of his or her sign, possessing all the faults and attributes associated with it. However, if the Moon and ascendant had been in Virgo then, whilst our subject would certainly display some of the Leo attributes or faults, it is more than likely that for the most part he or she would feel and behave more like a Virgoan.

As if life weren't complicated enough, this procedure must be carried through to take into account all the remaining planets. The position and signs of Mercury, Venus, Mars, Jupiter, Saturn, Uranus, Neptune and Pluto must all be discovered, plus the aspect formed from one planet to another. The calculation and interpretation of these movements by an astrologer will then produce an individual birth chart.

Because the heavens are constantly changing, people with identical charts are a very rare occurrence. Although it is not inconceivable that it could happen, this would mean that the two subjects were born not only on the same date and at the same time, but also in the same place. Should such an incident occur, then the deciding factors as to how these individuals would differ in their approach to life, love, career, financial prospects and so on, would be due to environmental and parental influence.

≈

Returning to our hypothetical Leo: our example with the rising Sun in Leo and Moon in Virgo may find it useful not only to read up on his or her Sun sign (Leo) but also to read the section dealing with Virgo (the Moon). Nevertheless, this does not invalidate Sun sign astrology. This is because of the great power the Sun possesses, and on any chart this planet plays an important role.

Belief in astrology does not necessarily mean believing in totally determined lives – that our actions are predestined and we have no control over our fate. What it does clearly show is that our lives run in cycles, for both good and bad and, with the aid of astrology, we can make the most of, or minimize, certain patterns and tendencies. How this is done is entirely up to the individual. For example, if you are in possession of the knowledge that you are about to experience a lucky few days or weeks, then you can make the most of them by pushing ahead with plans. You can also be better prepared for illness, misfortune, romantic upset and every adversity.

Astrology should be used as it was originally intended – as a guide, especially to character. In this direction it is invaluable and it can help us in all aspects of friendship, work and romance. It makes it easier for us to see ourselves as we really are and, what's more, as others see us. We can recognize both our own weaknesses and strengths and those of others. It can give us both outer confidence and inner peace.

In the following pages you will find personality profiles, an in-depth look at the year ahead from all possible angles including numerology, monthly and daily guides, your Sun sign partner, plus, and it is a big plus, information for those poor and confused creatures so often ignored who are born on 'the cusp' – at the beginning or the end of each sign.

Used wisely, astrology can help you through life. It is not intended to encourage complacency, since, in the final analysis, what you do with your life is up to you. This book will aid you in adopting the correct attitude to the year ahead and thus maximize your chances of success. Positive thinking is encouraged because this helps us to attract positive situations. Allow astrology to walk hand in hand with you and you will be increasing your chances of success and happiness.

≈

How Does
Astrology Work?

You often hear people say that there is no scientific explanation for astrology. However, astrological calculations may be explained in a very precise way, and they can be done by anyone with a little practice and a knowledge of the movement of stars and planets. It is the interpretations and conclusions drawn from these observations that are not necessarily consistent or verifiable, and, to be sure, predicted events do not always happen. Yet astrology has lasted in our culture for over 3,000 years, so there must be something in it!

So how can we explain astrology? Well, each individual birth sign has its own set of deep-seated characteristics, and an understanding of these can give you fresh insights into why you behave as you do. Reading an astrological interpretation, even if it is just to find out how, say, a new relationship might develop, means that you should think about yourself in a very deep way. But it is important to remember that the stars don't determine your fate. It is up to you to use them to the best advantage in any situation.

Although astrology, like many other 'alternative' practices such as homeopathy, dowsing and telepathy, cannot completely be explained, there have been convincing experiments that have shown that it works far more often than chance would allow. The best-known studies are those of the French statistician, Michel Gauquelin, whose results were checked by a professor at the University of London who declared, grudgingly, that 'there was something in it'.

An important aspect of astrology is to look at how the Sun and the Moon affect the natural world around us from day to day. For instance, the rise and fall of the tides is purely a result of the movement and position of the Moon relative to the Earth. If this massive magnetic pull can move the oceans of the Earth, what does it do to us? After all, we are, on average, over 60 per cent water!

When it comes to the ways in which the Sun may change the world, a whole book could be written on the subject. The influences we know about include day length, heat, light, solar storms, as well as magnetic, ultra-violet and many other forms of radiation. And all this from over 90 million miles away! For example, observation of birds has shown that before migration – governed by changes in the length of days – birds put on extra layers of fat, and that they experience a nocturnal restlessness shortly before setting off on their travels. I'm not suggesting that we put on weight and experience sleepless nights because of the time of year, but many people will tell you that different seasons affect them in different ways.

Another example from the natural world is a curious species of giant worm which lives in underground caverns in the South Pacific. Twice a year, as the Sun is rising and the tide is at its highest, these worms come to the surface of the ocean. The inhabitants of the islands consider them a great delicacy! There are so many instances of creatures on this planet responding to the influences of the Moon and the Sun that it is only common sense to wonder whether the position of other planets also has an affect, even if it is more subtle and less easy to identify.

Finally, we come to the question of how astrology might work in predicting future events. As we have seen, the planetary bodies are likely to affect us in all sorts of ways, both physically and mentally. Most often, subtle changes in the positions of the planets will cause slight changes in our emotional states and, of course, this will affect how we behave. By drawing up a chart based on precise birth times, and by using their intuition, some astrologers can make precise predictions about how planetary influences in the years ahead are likely to shape the life of an individual. Many people are very surprised at how well an astrologer seems to 'understand' them after reading a commentary on their birth chart!

Stranger still are the astrologers who appear to be able to predict future events many years before they happen. The most famous example of all is the 16th-century French astrologer, Nostradamus, who is well-known for having predicted the possibility of world destruction at the end of the last millennium. Don't worry, I think I can cheerfully put everyone's mind at rest by assuring you that the world will go on for a good many years yet. Although Nostradamus certainly made some very accurate predictions in his lifetime, his prophecies for our future are very obscure and are hotly disputed by all the experts. Mind you, it is quite clear that there are likely to be massive changes ahead. It is a possibility, for instance, that information may come to light about past civilizations, now at the bottom of the Mediterranean Sea: this will give us a good idea about how people once lived in the past, and pointers as to how we should live in the future. Try not to fear, dear reader. Astrology is a tool for us to use and if we use it wisely, no doubt we will survive with greater wisdom and a greater respect for our world and each other.

The Sun in Aquarius

You're like Alice/Alec in Wonderland, running through the forest making friends with all the creatures and asking a great many questions. Questions are to you what complaints are to a depressed person. You are probably the most frenetic person in the zodiac, and look upon life as a combination of Disneyland, the Planetarium and the Zoo.

'That's odd,' you say to yourself, shaking your head with a gleam in your eye. This means that you are impressed, enthralled, mystified and excited. You love unusual things which make other people turn their heads and wonder if they might be going momentarily mad.

The more peculiar incidents there are in your life, the better. One of your favourite things is to stay up all night analysing and speculating until in the morning; your eyes look like a proofreader's. Nothing would thrill you more than to be introduced to a Dracula look-alike whose teeth resemble weapons and whose pale-faced girlfriend has blood on her neck.

You thrive in a situation of mental challenge, and gravitate towards people who love constructive change as much as you do. The narrow-minded souls are those you want to avoid at

all costs, along with people who let their limitations enclose them. You're a free spirit whose versatility is hard to match. You love to take on a lot of things at once, and to deal in intellectually competitive situations that demand your attention.

In relationships, if you discover the person you felt so secure with was dishonest and unfaithful, the first thing you would do would be to sit down and find out why. While another person might yell, throw things or cry, you would calmly say – 'I just don't understand.' It's not that you don't have any feelings, it's just that in any situation, conflict or disaster, 'why' always takes precedence.

When communication stops flowing, you no longer see why a relationship should continue. Because your personality is basically non-attached, break-ups never worry you that much, although sadness may overcome you in solitary moments. You face endings as calmly as you face beginnings, but with less expectation or enthusiasm.

You are a fascinating person and an inspiration to those around you, even though they will never, in a lifetime, be able to fathom your feelings.

≈

The Year Ahead:
Overview

This year Pluto continues its journey through the fiery sign of Sagittarius, stimulating your faith in human nature, your impulsiveness, enthusiasm, wisdom, sense of perspective, exploration, versatility and joviality. However, from time to time you will be obsessed with the need to hang on to your precious freedom. Furthermore, you will feel a compelling need to be moving in the right direction.

Pluto will be drifting along in the area of your chart devoted to friends and acquaintances, so there's going to be a vital need for co-operation and friendship. On some occasions this could lead to rather odd alliances. You'll have the ability to influence friends, though it has to be said that during the year there may be sudden partings from your friends for various reasons.

During 2002 Neptune can be found in your own sign, and because of this you'll be much more responsive to social, political and philosophical stimulation, and those humanitarian ideals of yours are going to be especially strong.

You will have the power to theorize, but from time to time the planets will be inflating your love of independence, which could get out of hand. What's more, your mystical sense will be on the rampage, and you may do a certain amount of investigation into occult affairs, which will prove to be illuminating.

Your own planet, Uranus, will also be making its way through the air sign of Aquarius – your own sign – where it will be awakening originality, understanding and progressive thinking, while at the same time destroying sentimentality. This placing will make you more spirited and wayward, but you could become self-willed and perverse from time to time.

The position of Uranus will be encouraging inventiveness, ingenious thoughts and original and unconventional attitudes, as well as helping you to be a more curious liberal. There may be some sudden, unexpected and stimulating chances to travel, and you are certainly going to be more than usually popular with relatives and neighbours.

Uranus is the planet of the unexpected. Of course, this can be positive, but it can equally be extremely difficult, as there may be times when it produces sudden reversals of ideas which confuse everybody around.

Saturn – the planet that most of us seem, perhaps unfairly, to dread – will be making its way through Gemini all year. You will need to fight to develop some ordered thinking for a change. However, you will also need to be adaptable and versatile in your reasoning faculties, which won't be too difficult, because you will be far more accurate and observant in your thinking. Your mind may work a little bit slowly from time to time, but you'll get there in the end – providing, of course, that you avoid being tied down in any way.

Jupiter will be in Cancer until 1 August. For the most part this will ensure that you're hale and hearty where health matters are concerned. However, Jupiter is the 'greedy pig' of the zodiac, so you'll be strongly tempted into excesses this year.

≈

It is up to you to control them if you want to maintain your physical wellbeing. This shouldn't be very difficult, because when you set your mind to something, you invariably succeed.

Jupiter will be entering Leo on 2 August, where it will stay for the remainder of the year. Now, this is good news because that is the part of your chart devoted to your relationships, both professional and personal. There'll be many occasions when you'll feel it would be all right to pick the brains of other people and also ask them for a helping hand whenever necessary. Luckily, you're not the type who suffers from false pride as, for example, a Leo does (something which often holds this sign back). You love the whole big wide world and you naturally assume it loves you – and, for the most part, it does.

≈

Career Year

You're not the type of person who wants a great deal of power; however, you do demand the freedom to do as you please, without constant interference. Because you have a strong dislike of controlling structures, you're often happier working on your own. Your mind is like that of a mad scientist who sleeps in his laboratory so that he won't miss anything.

Although you enjoy your creature comforts, along with those priceless little gadgets, you don't need them enough to spend your life working in order to get them.

Success, for you, is the mental gratification that comes from discoveries, break-throughs, the feeling of progress or the unfolding of a truth. You must be stimulated by what you are doing in order to consider the undertaking successful. When a certain kind of work bores you, it leaves you unmoved and lacking in motivation.

Because you're idealistic about what you do, you are sometimes willing to sacrifice financial rewards for greater personal satisfaction. You're easily taken in by schemes that are not particularly security-oriented yet prove to be some kind of adventure.

You hate to feel you are being tied down to any work situation, especially when you can't see beyond the burdens it imposes. Therefore, the greatest success for you is doing your own thing and generally getting paid fairly for it. When you wake up in the morning to what you consider a consuming interest rather than a job, you're on the road to the kind of success you've always been searching for.

You have a scientific mind and a mathematical nature (other aspects willing, of course). Therefore, anything from nuclear physics to computers or accounting could appeal to you. Medicine is also a distinct possibility, or perhaps scientific research or psychiatry.

Since your mind is original, independent and often far beyond its time, the chances are you can invent a few new professions to suit yourself. At least one of them might be located on another planet; another could be an inter-planetary computer system that runs on thought. As long as your thoughts keep coming, universal progress will never grind to a halt.

The planet that rules work matters for you is Pluto, that heavenly body which represents change and upheaval. Therefore, where work is concerned it's unlikely that you'll be bored for very long: if you are, you'll simply move on.

This year, Pluto will be making its way through Sagittarius for the entire year. This is the area of your chart devoted to friends and acquaintances. Therefore, it seems that these people are going to be pivotal to your successes during 2002; it will definitely be who you know and not what you know that counts.

However, between 20 March and 25 August Pluto will be in retrograde movement. Because of this, a certain amount of frustration is likely. However, with any luck, other planetary movements during this time may aid and abet you. For details of when this is likely to happen, have a look at the monthly and daily guides.

≈

Money Year

You're one of those people who doesn't really value money for its own sake; however, it certainly helps you to do the impromptu things that pop into your head when you are bored. You're not the type to hoard your cash under your mattress and count it every full Moon. At the same time, you have the ability to think far ahead, which means you'll have your spending money all ready for your first trip to Pluto.

You do appreciate the finer things in life and have a level of practicality that people who love you are constantly surprised at. You may be up in the air most of the time, but you're very down to earth when it comes to cash. There's no doubt about it, you're certainly full of surprises.

In general, you are as generous as Father Christmas. When the restaurant bill comes, you grab it. If you're a highly intelligent Aquarian, the only value you can find in money is in giving it away. It makes you feel happy to give, even if the object of your charity needs the money less than you do. Money is never going to control you, because you see its value as transient. Whatever you decide to do with it, you make sure that you enjoy it, even if it means getting rid of it.

So how are you likely to fare during the year ahead?

Well, finances seem to be relatively healthy and you can generate as much money as you want through your originality and your bright ideas, so there's very little for you to worry about – until Neptune decides to go into retrograde movement from 13 May until 19 October. This is an indecently long time, you've got to admit. So, during this large portion of the year you'll need to be extremely careful. If you're going to be ripped off by shoddy goods, or get an inflated idea of how much is left in the bank and spend accordingly, then it's going to be during this time. It's up to you to stay as vigilant as you can. Mind you, you've got to admit you're always a little bit casual where cash matters are concerned, so what's new really?

Luckily, at least, Neptune resumes direct movement on 20 October, just in time for Christmas. Once this occurs, all the monies that have been owing to you will suddenly all come in at once. The only problem is, of course, that you may decide that you can spend without thinking of the future – not a good idea. Try to let the stars work for you and be cautious during the times that I have mentioned. If in general you can keep your head, then there'll be no reason why this year should be any worse than any other. Mind you, it may not be any better either.

For further information you will need to refer to the monthly and daily guides.

≈

Love and Sex Year

When it comes to romance, you are a truly independent sort of person; you create a comfortable space between yourself and others, and stay at a safe distance. Therefore, your attitude towards love is just like you – unconventional and different.

The less you see of your lovers, the more you want them. You stay away from predatory people who might close in and cut you off from the feeling of freedom that is so precious to you.

Soft lights and mood music don't move you half as much as somebody who is intelligent to talk to. The more interests they have, the better, since you are seeking the mental stimulation that arises from a vital, inquisitive person. Because your attitude towards love is more cerebral than emotional, you have to like the idea of the person before you can come to the point of loving. Admiration is a key factor to your emotional make-up: the more someone gives you reason to feel it, the more responsive you spontaneously become.

Basically you're looking for someone to share your passion for photography, body-painting and nuclear physics. Even better, you'd like someone who also has many passions of their own to share with you. Falling in love with an

Aquarian means having a mind so stimulated that the body is sometimes forgotten.

Even when you're in love, you are detached and freedom-loving, which may madden or confuse a possessive partner. You probably see your love as your best friend and partner, and find flowery language and romanticism far too excessive. You find so much drama and excitement in the details of daily life that you don't feel the need to impose B-movie standards on your relationships.

Because you are idealistic, you're also a romantic in your idiosyncratic way. However, most people neither see this nor understand it. When you do love, you embrace all the person's faults and virtues, without illusion and without compulsion to reform them. When an admirer seems to be encroaching on your private space, with no intention of moving, you'll say in a characteristically Aquarian way, 'Let's be friends.'

However, how are you likely to fare during this particular year?

Well, the planet which rules the relationship area to your life is the Sun. This is a fast-moving planet, which is probably why you get through an indecent number of lovers in any given year.

From 1 to 19 January, the Sun will be sizzling along in the earthy sign of Capricorn, a rather secretive part of your chart. Oh dear, it looks as if you could become involved with people who are not being honest with you, or perhaps taking you for a ride. This would hurt quite badly, though you'd never admit it. Be alert.

From 20 January to 18 February, the Sun will be in your sign, giving you the utmost confidence and making you very attractive. Make sure you keep a high profile, and don't be suspicious. Give others a chance and maybe, just maybe, you might meet someone very special.

From 19 February to 20 March, the Sun will be in Pisces, the area of your chart devoted to money. It's unlikely that you're thinking seriously about 'naming the day'.

From 21 March to 19 April, the Sun coasts along in Aries. This seems to be a good period because it suits your mood and your character, as you'll be prepared to meet as many people as possible and get the most out of each relationship, though hopefully you won't allow that other person to believe for one moment that you're thinking of getting married – that would be to mislead them.

From 20 April to 20 May, the Sun will be coasting along in earthy Taurus. At this time you may be looking for somebody you can rely on, somebody who will always be in your corner, but after a short while, of course, you'll get bored with this and start looking around. However, if you are unfaithful I'm afraid you're likely to be found out, and then there'll be an almighty explosion.

From 21 May to 21 June, the Sun will be in Gemini. This is more your cup of tea, because you'll be quite happy to take on as many admirers as possible. There does seem to be a great deal of fun in your chart at this time, so it's likely that the other person is as carefree as you. It's certainly a time you won't forget for a while, even if it doesn't lead up the aisle, which you're not thinking of anyway.

From 22 June to 22 July the Sun will be in Cancer, so new love interests may be found while you go about your daily duties. Mind you, although this might generate a certain amount of passion, once more it doesn't seem to last for long. Maybe you or the other person simply aren't taking it seriously.

From 23 July to 22 August, the Sun is in Leo, your opposite number. All of your relationships, be they personal, professional, with relatives or with new loves, are going to be flourishing like crazy. You're enjoying yourself but, of course, you're still not thinking of making a commitment.

From 23 August to 22 September, the Sun will be in Virgo, so it is the people who share your resources, such as your family or your professional partners, who may be supplying some interesting introductions. Once more, however, it doesn't look as if anything's going to last for very long.

From 23 September to 23 October, the Sun will be in Libra; because of this you may be attracted to people with strange-sounding names and accents. If you're taking a late holiday, you can be quite sure to be positively surrounded by admirers, but then again you're still valuing your freedom above anything else.

From 24 October to 21 November the Sun is in Scorpio, therefore it is those you meet while going about your professional duties who may supply some kind of either sex interest or love interest, on a temporary basis anyway. It doesn't look as if anything permanent is developing yet.

From 22 November to 21 December the Sun will be drifting along in the fiery sign of Sagittarius, the area of your chart devoted to friends, acquaintances and club activities. Indirectly or directly, these are the avenues through which you'll be meeting your new admirers.

From 22 December to the end of the year the Sun will be in Capricorn. Oh dear, do take care. It's quite likely that others may be anything but straightforward and honest with you, and you're not the sort of person who is prepared to take on board a threesome. In other words, your admirer might like the thought of this kind of thing, but you're far too straightforward and honest to deal with it.

So, Aquarius, it's certainly going to be an up and down year, but then that's the way you like it. If you want further information on the best time to act and find romance, then please refer to the monthly and daily guides.

≈

Health and Diet Year

Your nervous system is on so high a frequency that dogs start howling whenever you walk past. Because of your over-worked head, insomnia is often a problem, leading to physical exhaustion and sometimes depression.

An erratic nature and emotional instability are typical Aquarian pathologies, but they can easily be avoided with rest and regular meditation. Prolonged, unrelieved stress can set your entire nervous system up for a breakdown that begins insidiously, when you are least aware of it.

Muscular spasms can also cause discomfort if you are the type who neglects the needs of your body in the interests of the activities of the mind. Regular exercise, especially yoga, is an excellent way to keep your body young and functioning smoothly.

Later in life, high blood pressure may menace your system, so avoid any excessive use of salt, as well as foods high in cholesterol. A course of deep breathing, regularly applied, can ultimately slow down your heartbeat and pro-long your life.

Finally, when an onslaught of nervous energy starts to make you irritable, calcium and magnesium tablets can slow you down and cool you off. Because they have a calming effect, a regular morning dose with your yoghurt and orange juice can prove more than worthwhile in the long run, especially when you notice that the dogs have shut up and started to stare at you in silence.

However, what are the pros and cons of the year 2002?

Well, it's nice to be able to tell you that for the most part you will be disgustingly healthy. You haven't got time for sitting around and giving in to a bout of the sneezes or a headache, or even a cramp; you want to be out in the world because you're quite sure you're missing out, and you're usually right. Because of this attitude it seems fitting that it is the Moon we must look to for your state of health. When it is full, you might be feeling temporarily under the weather, but that doesn't matter too much because the full Moon doesn't last that long. Conversely, when there is a nice new Moon you're feeling decidedly chipper, ready to get stuck in to life and enjoy it as much as possible. Therefore, use this little book in order to discover when the new and full Moons occur, so that you are pre-warned as to how to use them to best effect.

During January there's a beautiful new Moon in the sign of Capricorn on the 13th, so you're certainly looking good, feeling great and can take on literally anything or anyone, even with both hands tied behind your back. However, on 28 January there's a full Moon in your opposite sign of Leo. This could bring you down, draining your energy and making you exaggerate problems, so take care.

On 12 February the new Moon occurs in your own sign. You can do no wrong at this time, and this gives you not only confidence, but a secret feeling of wellbeing. You therefore have reason to be happy. The full Moon occurs on 27 February in Virgo. You'll be unenthusiastic about work. You know this is the wrong thing to do, but you simply can't stir yourself no matter how hard you try, so get some relaxation in the evenings.

On 14 March, there's a beautiful new Moon in the sign of Pisces. There could be some financial luck, which will certainly be cheering you up no end. Unfortunately, the full Moon on 28 March in Libra affects your mind so that you exaggerate everything beyond all belief – try to control this.

On 12 April there's a nice new Moon in Aries. New friends and club activities cheer you up no end, and team work is also well starred. However, the full Moon on 27 April in Scorpio means there are problems at work, and this will bring you down. Don't exaggerate them beyond belief.

During May the new Moon occurs on the 12th in Taurus. You're getting on with those at home like a house on fire. The full Moon occurs on 26 May in Taurus; you will be feeling quite outgoing, so make the best of this time and get out there and meet up with your friends and acquaintances.

On 10 June, the new Moon occurs in the air sign of Gemini. This is a good time for foreign affairs and travel. However, the full Moon of the 24th is in Capricorn, the secretive part of your chart. You may be feeling uneasy, though you may not know the reason why – now you do.

During July, the new Moon occurs in Cancer on the 10th, a good time for routine work and improving your relationships with workmates. However, there is a full Moon on the 22nd in your own sign, which could make you feel unenthusiastic and rather negative, so don't do anything important.

On 7 September the new Moon occurs in Virgo. This is the time to ask for favours from workmates. You're feeling good and looking good and no one can resist you. However, the full Moon on the 21st in Pisces could make for some financial

≈

problems, so try to budget accordingly – though this is difficult for you, I do appreciate.

There is a new Moon in airy Libra on 6 October. This is not the time to be too ambitious. If you take too much on, you will only make mistakes and stress yourself out. On 21 October the full Moon is in Aries; you should take care when you are on the go. Leave plenty of time for appointments and any plans you have made, or you may find yourself in a muddle – and this can only be frustrating.

On 4 November the new Moon occurs in Scorpio, the zenith point of your chart. There's good news in connection with your job. However, the full Moon on the 20th occurs in Taurus, so there may be arguments on the home front. Try to act as 'peace-maker'.

During December, the new Moon occurs on the 4th in Sagittarius, so you're meeting new friends, visiting clubs and thoroughly enjoying yourself. Lastly, the full Moon during December occurs on the 19th, in Gemini. Matters related to children and love affairs could go 'awry'.

As you go through this little book month by month and day by day, you'll be reminded of all the new and full Moons.

≋

Numerology Year

In order to discover the number of any year you are interested in, your 'individual year number', first take your birth date, day and month, and add this to the year you are interested in, be it in the past or in the future. As an example, say you were born on 13 August and the year you are interested in is 2002:

$$
\begin{array}{r}
13 \\
+ \quad 8 \\
+ \quad 2002 \\
\hline
2023
\end{array}
$$

Then, write down $2 + 0 + 2 + 3$ and you will discover this equals 7. This means that your year number is 7. If the number adds up to more than 9, add these two digits together.

You can experiment with this method by taking any year from your past and following this guide to find whether or not numerology works out for you.

The guide is perennial and applicable to all Sun signs: you can look up years for your friends as well as for yourself. Use it to discover general trends ahead, the way you should be approaching a chosen period and how you can make the most of the future.

Individual Year Number 1

General Feel

A time for being more self-sufficient and one when you should be ready to really go for it. All opportunities must be snapped up, after careful consideration. Also an excellent time for laying down the foundations for future success in all areas.

Definition

Because this is the number 1 individual year, you will have the chance to start again in many areas of life. The emphasis will be upon the new; there will be fresh faces in your life, more opportunities and perhaps even new experiences. If you were born on either the 1st, 19th or 28th and were born under the sign of Aries or Leo then this will be an extremely important time. It is crucial during this cycle that you are prepared to go it alone, push back horizons and generally open up your mind. Time also for playing the leader or pioneer wherever necessary. If you have a hobby that you wish to turn into a business, or maybe you simply wish to introduce other people to your ideas and plans, then do so whilst experiencing this individual cycle. A great period too for laying down plans for long-term future gains. Therefore, make sure you do your homework well and you will reap the rewards at a later date.

Relationships

This is an ideal period for forming new bonds, perhaps business relationships, new friends and new loves too. You will be attracted to those in high positions and with strong personalities. There may also be an emphasis on bonding with people a good deal younger than yourself. If you are already in a long-standing relationship, then it is time to clear away the dead wood between you which may have been causing misunderstandings and unhappiness. Whether in love or business, you will find those who are born under the sign of Aries, Leo or Aquarius far more common in your life, also those born on the following dates: 1st, 4th, 9th, 10th, 13th, 18th, 19th, 22nd and 28th. The most important months for this individual year, when you are likely to meet up with those who have a strong influence on you, are January, May, July and October.

Career

It is likely that you have been wanting to break free and to explore fresh horizons in your career and this is definitely a year for doing so. Because you are in a fighting mood, and because your decision-making qualities as well as your leadership qualities are foremost, it will be an easy matter for you to find assistance as well as to impress other people. Major professional changes are likely and you will also feel more independent within your existing job. Should you want times for making important career moves, then choose Mondays or Tuesdays. These are good days for pushing your luck and presenting your ideas well. Changes connected with your career are going to be more likely during April, May, July and September.

Health

If you have forgotten the name of your doctor or dentist, then this is the year to start regular checkups. A time too when people of a certain age are likely to start wearing glasses. The emphasis seems to be on the eyes. Start a good health regime. This will help you cope with any adverse events that almost assuredly lie ahead. The important months for your own health as well as for loved ones are March, May and August.

Individual Year Number 2

General Feel
You will find it far easier to relate to other people.

Definition
What you will need during this cycle is diplomacy, cooperation and the ability to put yourself in someone else's shoes. Whatever you began last year will now begin to show signs of progress. However, don't expect miracles; changes are going to be slow rather than at the speed of light. Changes will be taking place all around you. It is possible too that you will be considering moving from one area to another, maybe even to another country. There is a lively feel about domesticity and in relationships with the opposite sex too. This is going to be a marvellous year for making things come true and asking for favours. However, on no account should you force yourself and your opinions on other people. A spoonful of honey is going to get you a good deal further than a spoonful of vinegar. If you are born under the sign of Cancer or Taurus, or if your birthday falls on the 2nd, 11th, 20th or 29th, then this year is going to be full of major events.

Relationships
You need to associate with other people far more than is usually the case – perhaps out of necessity. The emphasis is on love, friendship and professional partnerships. The opposite

sex will be much more prepared to get involved in your life than is normally the case. This year you have a far greater chance of becoming engaged or married, and there is likely to be a lovely addition both to your family and to the families of your friends and those closest to you. The instinctive and caring side to your personality is going to be strong and very obvious. You will quickly discover that you will be particularly touchy and sensitive to things that other people say. Further, you will find those born under the sign of Cancer, Taurus and Libra entering your life far more than is usually the case. This also applies to those who are born on the 2nd, 6th, 7th, 11th, 15th, 20th, 24th, 25th or 29th of the month.

Romantic and family events are likely to be emphasized during April, June and September.

Career

There is a strong theme of change here, but there is no point in having a panic attack about that because, after all, life is about change. However, in this particular individual year any transformation or upheaval is likely to be of an internal nature, such as at your place of work, rather than external. You may find your company is moving from one area to another, or perhaps there are changes between departments. Quite obviously then, the most important thing for you to do in order to make your life easy is to be adaptable. There is a strong possibility too that you may be given added responsibility. Do not flinch as this will bring in extra reward.

If you are thinking of searching for employment this year, then try to arrange all meetings and negotiations on Monday and Friday. These are good days for asking for favours or rises too. The best months are March, April, June, August, and December. All these are important times for change.

≈

Health

This individual cycle emphasizes stomach problems. The important thing for you is to eat sensibly, rather than go on a crash diet, for example – this could be detrimental. If you are female then you would be wise to have a checkup at least once during the year ahead just to be sure you can continue to enjoy good health. All should be discriminating when dining out. Check cutlery, and take care that food has not been partially cooked. Furthermore, emotional stress could get you down, but only if you allow it. Provided you set aside some periods of relaxation in each day when you can close your eyes and let everything drift away, you will have little to worry about. When it comes to diet, be sure that the emphasis is on nutrition, rather than fighting the flab. Perhaps it would be a good idea to become less weight conscious during this period and let your body find its natural ideal weight on its own. The months of February, April, July and November may show health changes in some way. Common sense is your best guide during this year.

Individual Year Number 3

General Feel

You are going to be at your most creative and imaginative during this time. There is a theme of expansion and growth and you will want to polish up your self-image in order to make the 'big impression'.

Definition

It is a good year for reaching out, for expansion. Social and artistic developments should be interesting as well as profitable and this will help to promote happiness. There will be a

strong urge in you to improve yourself – either your image or
your reputation or, perhaps, your mind. Your popularity soars
through the ceiling and this delights you. Involving yourself
with something creative brings increased success plus a good
deal of satisfaction. However, it is imperative that you keep
yourself in a positive mood. This will attract attention and
appreciation of all your talents. Projects which were begun
two years ago are likely to be bearing fruit this year. If you are
born under the sign of Pisces or Sagittarius, or your birthday
falls on the 3rd, 12th, 21st or 30th, then this year is going to be
particularly special and successful.

Relationships

There is a happy-go-lucky feel about all your relationships
and you are in a flirty, fancy-free mood. Heaven help anyone
trying to catch you during the next twelve months: they will
need to get their skates on. Relationships are likely to be lighthearted and fun rather than heavy going. It is possible too
that you will find yourself with those who are younger than
you, particularly those born under the signs of Pisces and
Sagittarius, and those whose birth dates add up to 3, 6 or 9.
Your individual cycle shows important months for relationships are March, May, August and December.

Career

As I discussed earlier, this individual number is one that suggests branching out and personal growth, so be ready to take
on anything new. Not surprisingly, your career prospects look
bright and shiny. You are definitely going to be more ambitious and must keep up that positive façade and attract
opportunities. Avoid taking obligations too lightly; it is
important that you adopt a conscientious approach to all your

≈

responsibilities. You may take on a fresh course of learning or look for a new job, and the important days for doing so would be on Thursday and Friday: these are definitely your best days. This is particularly true in the months of February, March, May, July and November: expect expansion in your life and take a chance during these times.

Health

Because you are likely to be out and about painting the town all the colours of the rainbow, it is likely that health problems could come through over-indulgence or perhaps tiredness. However, if you must have some health problems, I suppose these are the best ones to experience, because they are under your control. There is also a possibility that you may get a little fraught over work, which may result in some emotional scenes. However, you are sensible enough to realize they should not be taken too seriously. If you are prone to skin allergies, then these too could be giving you problems during this particular year. The best advice you can follow is not to go to extremes that will affect your body or your mind. It is all very well to have fun, but after a while too much of it affects not only your health but also the degree of enjoyment you experience. Take extra care between January and March, and June and October, especially where these are winter months for you.

Individual Year Number 4

General Feel

It is back to basics this year. Do not build on shaky foundations. Get yourself organized and be prepared to work a little harder than you usually do and you will come through without any great difficulty.

Definition

It is imperative that you have a grand plan. Do not simply rush off without considering the consequences, and avoid dabbling of any kind. It is likely too that you will be gathering more responsibility and on occasions this could lead you to feeling unappreciated, claustrophobic and perhaps over-burdened in some ways. Although it is true to say that this cycle in your individual life tends to bring about a certain amount of limitation, whether this be on the personal, the psychological or the financial side of life, you now have the chance to get yourself together and to build on more solid foundations. Security is definitely your key word at this time. When it comes to any project, job or plan, it is important that you ask the right questions. In other words, do your homework and do not rush blindly into anything. That would be a dis-aster. If you are an Aquarius, a Leo or a Gemini or you are born on the 4th, 13th, 22nd, or the 31st of any month, this individual year will be extremely important and long remembered.

Relationships

You will find that it is the eccentric, the unusual, the uncon-ventional and the downright odd that will be drawn into your life during this particular cycle. It is also strongly possible that people you have not met for some time may be re-entering your circle and an older person or somebody outside your own social or perhaps religious background will be drawn to you too. When it comes to the romantic side of life, again you are drawn to that which is different from usual. You may even form a relationship with someone who comes from a totally different background, perhaps from far away. Something unusual about them stimulates and excites you. Gemini, Leo and Aquarius are your likely favourites, as well as anyone whose birth number adds up to 1, 4, 5 or 7. Certainly the most exciting months for romance are going to be February, April, July and November. Make sure then that you socialize a lot during these particular times, and be ready for literally anything.

Career

Once more we have the theme of the unusual and different in this area of life. You may be plodding along in the same old rut when suddenly lightning strikes and you find yourself besieged by offers from other people and, in a panic, not quite sure what to do. There may be a period when nothing particular seems to be going on when, to your astonishment, you are given a promotion or some exciting challenge. Literally anything can happen in this particular cycle of your life. The individual year 4 also inclines towards added responsibilities and it is important that you do not off-load them onto other people or cringe in fear. They will eventually pay off and in the meantime you will be gaining in experience and paving the way for greater success in the future. When you want to arrange any kind of meeting, negotiation or perhaps ask for a favour at work, then try to do so on a Monday or a Wednesday for the luckiest results. January, February, April, October and November are certainly the months when you must play the opportunist and be ready to say yes to anything that comes your way.

Health

The biggest problems that you will have to face this year are caused by stress, so it is important that you attend to your diet and take life as philosophically as possible, as well as being ready to adapt to changing conditions. You are likely to find that people you thought you knew well are acting out of character and this throws you off balance. Take care, too, when visiting the doctor. Remember that you are dealing with a human being and that doctors, like the rest of us, can make mistakes. Unless you are 100 per cent satisfied then go for a second opinion over anything important. Try to be sceptical about yourself because you are going to be a good deal more moody than usual. The times that need special attention are February, May, September and November. If any of these months fall in the winter part of your year, then wrap up well and dose up on vitamin C.

Individual Year Number 5

General Feel

There will be many more opportunities for you to get out and about, and travel is certainly going to be playing a large part in your year. Change, too, must be expected and even embraced – after all, it is part of life. You will have more free time and choices, so all in all things look promising.

Definition

It is possible that you tried previously to get something off the launchpad, but for one reason or another it simply didn't happen. Luckily, you now get a chance to renew those old plans and put them into action. You are certainly going to feel that things are changing for the better in all areas. You will be more actively involved with the public and enjoy a certain amount of attention and publicity. You may have failed in the past but this year mistakes will be easier to accept and learn from; you are going to find yourself both physically and mentally more in tune with your environment and with those you care about than ever before. If you are a Gemini or a Virgo or are born on the 5th, 14th or 23rd, then this is going to be a period of major importance for you and you must be ready to take advantage of this.

Relationships

Lucky you! Your sexual magnetism goes through the ceiling and you will be involved in many relationships during the year ahead. You have that extra charisma about you which will be attracting others and you can look forward to being choosy. There will be an inclination to be drawn to those who are considerably younger than yourself. It is likely too that you will find that those born under the signs of Taurus, Gemini, Virgo and Libra as well as those whose birth date adds up to 2, 5 or 6 will play an important part in your year. The months for attracting others in a big way are January, March, June, October and December.

Career

This is considered by all numerologists as being one of the best numbers for self-improvement in all areas, but particularly on the professional front. It will be relatively easy for you to sell your ideas and yourself, as well as to push your skills and expertise under the noses of other people. They will certainly sit up and take notice. Clearly, then, this is a time for you to view the world as your oyster and to get out there and grab your piece of the action. You have increased confidence and should be able to get exactly what you want. Friday and Wednesday are perhaps the best days if looking for a job or going to negotiations or interviews, or in fact for generally pushing yourself into the limelight. Watch out for March, May, September, October or December. Something of great importance could pop up at this time. There will certainly be a chance for advancement; whether you take it or not is, of course, entirely up to you.

Health

Getting a good night's rest could be your problem during the year ahead, since that mind of yours is positively buzzing and won't let you rest. Try turning your brain off at bedtime, otherwise you will finish up irritable and exhausted. Try to take things a step at a time without rushing around. Meditation may help you to relax and do more for your physical wellbeing than anything else. Because this is an extremely active year, you will need to do some careful planning so that you can cope with ease rather than rushing around like a demented mayfly. Furthermore, try to avoid going over the top with alcohol, food, sex, gambling or anything which could be described as a 'quick fix'. During January, April, August and October, watch yourself a bit, you could do with some pampering, particularly if these happen to be winter months for you.

Individual Year Number 6

General Feel

There is likely to be increased responsibility and activity within your domestic life. There will be many occasions when you will be helping loved ones and your sense of duty is going to be strong.

Definition

Activities for the most part are likely to be centred around property, family, loved ones, romance and your home. Your artistic appreciation will be good and you will be drawn to anything that is colourful and beautiful, and possessions that have a strong appeal to your eye or even your ear. Where domesticity is concerned, there is a strong suggestion that you may move out of one home into another. This is an excellent time, too, for self-education, for branching out, for graduating, for taking on some extra courses – whether simply to improve your appearance or to improve your mind. When it comes to your social life you are inundated with chances to attend events. You are going to be a real social butterfly, flitting from scene to scene and enjoying yourself thoroughly. Try to accept nine out of ten invitations that come your way because they bring with them chances of advancement. If you are born on the 6th, 15th or 24th, or should your birth sign be Taurus, Libra or Cancer, then this year will be long remembered as a very positive one.

Relationships

When it comes to love, sex and romance the individual year 6 is perhaps the most successful. It is a time for being swept off your feet, for becoming engaged or even getting married. On the more negative side, perhaps, there could be separation and divorce. However, the latter can be avoided, provided you are prepared to sit down and communicate properly. There is an emphasis too on pregnancy and birth, or changes in existing relationships. Circumstances will be sweeping you along. If you are born under the sign of Taurus, Cancer or Libra, then it is even more likely that this will be a major year for you, as well as for those born on dates adding up to 6, 3 or 2. The most memorable months of your year are going to be February, May, September and November. Grab all opportunities to enjoy yourself and improve your relationships during these periods.

Career

A good year for this side of life too, with the chances of promotion and recognition for past efforts all coming your way. You will be able to improve your position in life even though it is likely that recently you have been disappointed. On the cash front, big rewards will come flooding in mainly because you are prepared to fulfil your obligations and commitments without complaint or protest. Other people will appreciate all the efforts you have put in, so plod along and you will find your efforts will not have been in vain. Perversely, if you are looking for a job or setting up an interview, negotiation or a meeting, or simply want to advertise your talents in some way, then your best days for doing so are Monday, Thursday and Friday. Long-term opportunities are very strong during the months of February, April, August, September and November. These are the key periods for pushing yourself up the ladder of success.

Health

If you are to experience any problems of a physical nature during this year, then they could be tied up with the throat, nose or the tonsils, plus the upper parts of the body. Basically, what you need to stay healthy during this year is plenty of sunlight, moderate exercise, fresh air and changes of scene. Escape to the coast if this is at all possible. The months for being particularly watchful are March, July, September and December. Think twice before doing anything during these times and there is no reason why you shouldn't stay hale and hearty for the whole year.

≈

Individual Year Number 7

General Feel

A year for inner growth and for finding out what really makes you tick and what you need to make you happy. Self-awareness and discovery are all emphasized during the individual year 7.

Definition

You will be provided with the opportunity to place as much emphasis as possible on your personal life and your own well-being. There will be many occasions when you will find yourself analysing your past motives and actions, and giving more attention to your own personal needs, goals and desires. There will also be many occasions when you will want to escape any kind of confusion, muddle or noise; time spent alone will not be wasted. This will give you the chance to meditate and also to examine exactly where you have come to so far, and where you want to go in the future. It is important you make up your mind what you want out of this particular year because once you have done so you will attain those ambitions. Failure to do this could mean you end up chasing your own tail and that is a pure waste of time and energy. You will also discover that secrets about yourself and other people could be surfacing during this year. If you are born under the sign of Pisces or Cancer, or on the 7th, 16th or 25th of the month, then this year will be especially wonderful.

Relationships

It has to be said from the word go that this is not the best year for romantic interest. A strong need for contemplation will mean spending time on your own. Any romance that does develop this year may not live up to your expectations, but,

providing you are prepared to take things as they come without jumping to conclusions, then you will enjoy yourself
without getting hurt. Decide exactly what it is you have in
mind and then go for it. Romantic interests this year are likely
to be with people who are born on dates that add up to 2, 4 or
7, or with people born under the sign of Cancer or Pisces.
Watch for romantic opportunities during January, April,
August and October.

Career

When we pass through this particular individual cycle, two
things in life tend to occur: retirement from the limelight, and
a general slowing down, perhaps by taking leave of absence
or maybe retraining in some way. It is likely too that you will
become more aware of your own occupational expertise and
skills – you will begin to understand your true purpose in life
and will feel much more enlightened. Long-sought-after goals
begin to come to life if you have been drifting of late. The best
attitude to have throughout this year is an exploratory one
when it comes to your work. If you want to set up negotiations, interviews or meetings, arrange them for Monday or
Friday. In fact, any favours you seek should be tackled on
these days. January, March, July, August, October and
December are particularly good for self-advancement.

Health

Since, in comparison to previous years, this is a rather quiet
time, health problems are likely to be minor. Some will possibly
come through irritation or worry and the best thing to do is to
attempt to remain meditative and calm. This state of mind will
bring positive results. Failure to do so may create unnecessary
problems by allowing your imagination to run completely out

of control. You need time this year to restore, recuperate and
contemplate. Any health changes that do occur are likely to
happen in February, June, August and November.

Individual Year Number 8

General Feel
This is going to be a time for success, for making important
moves and changes, a time when you may gain power and
certainly one when your talents are going to be recognized.

Definition
This individual year gives you the chance to 'think big';
it is a time when you can occupy the limelight and wield
power. If you were born on the 8th, 17th or 26th of the
month or come under the sign of Capricorn, pay attention
to this year and make sure you make the most of it.
You should develop greater maturity and discover a true
feeling of faith and destiny, both in yourself and in events
that occur. This part of the cycle is connected with career,
ambition and money, but debts from the past will have to
be repaid. For example, an old responsibility or debt that
you may have avoided in past years may reappear to haunt
you. However, whatever you do with these twelve months,
aim high – think big, think success and above all be
positive.

Relationships
This particular individual year is one which is strongly
connected with birth, divorce and marriage – most of the land-
marks we experience in life, in fact. Love-wise, those who are
more experienced or older than you, or people of power,

authority, influence or wealth, will be very attractive. This year will be putting you back in touch with those from your past – old friends, comrades, associates, and even romances from long ago crop up once more. You should not experience any great problems romantically this year, especially if you are dealing with Capricorns or Librans, or with those whose date of birth adds up to 8, 6 or 3. The best months for romance to develop are likely to be March, July, September and December.

Career

The number 8 year is generally believed to be the best one when it comes to bringing in cash. It is also good for asking for a rise or achieving promotion or authority over other people. This is your year for basking in the limelight of success, the result perhaps of your past efforts. Now you will be rewarded. Financial success is all but guaranteed, provided you keep faith with your ambitions and yourself. It is important that you set major goals for yourself and work slowly towards them. You will be surprised how easily they are fulfilled. Conversely, if you are looking for work, then do set up interviews, negotiations and meetings, preferably on Saturday, Thursday or Friday, which are your luckiest days. Also watch out for chances to do yourself a bit of good during February, June, July, September and November.

Health

You can avoid most health problems, particularly headaches, constipation or liver problems, by avoiding depression and feelings of loneliness. It is important when these descend that you keep yourself busy enough not to dwell on them. When it comes to receiving attention from the medical profession you would be well advised to get a second opinion. Eat wisely, try to

≈

keep a positive and enthusiastic outlook on life and all will be well. Periods which need special care are January, May, July and October. Therefore, if these months fall during the winter part of your year, wrap up well and dose yourself with vitamins.

Individual Year Number 9

General Feel
A time for tying up loose ends. Wishes are likely to be fulfilled and matters brought to swift conclusions. Inspiration runs amok. Much travel is likely.

Definition
The number 9 individual year is perhaps the most successful of all. It tends to represent the completion of matters and affairs, whether in work, business, or personal affairs. Your ability to let go of habits, people and negative circumstances or situations, that may have been holding you back, is strong. The sympathetic and humane side to your character also surfaces and you learn to give more freely of yourself without expecting anything in return. Any good deeds that you do will certainly be well rewarded in terms of satisfaction, and perhaps financially, too. If you are born under the sign of Aries or Scorpio, or on the 9th, 18th or 27th of the month, this is certainly going to be an all-important year.

Relationships
The individual year 9 is a cycle which gives appeal as well as influence. Because of this, you will be getting emotionally tied up with members of the opposite sex who may be outside your usual cultural or ethnic group. The reason for this is that this particular number relates to humanity and of course this

tends to quash ignorance, pride and bigotry. You also discover that Aries, Leo and Scorpio people are going to be much more evident in your domestic affairs, as well as those whose birth dates add up to 9, 3 or 1. The important months for relationships are February, June, August and November. These will be extremely hectic and eventful from a romantic viewpoint and there are times when you could be swept off your feet.

Career

This is a year which will help to make many of your dreams and ambitions come true. Furthermore, it is an excellent time for success if you are involved in marketing your skills, talents and expertise more widely. You may be thinking of expanding abroad for example and, if so, this is certainly a good idea. You will find that harmony and cooperation with your fellow workers are easier than before and this will help your dreams and ambitions. The best days for you if you want to line up meetings or negotiations are going to be Tuesdays and Thursdays, and this also applies if you are looking for employment or want a special day for doing something of an ambitious nature. Employment or business changes could also feature during January, May, June, August and October.

Health

The only physical problems you may have during this particular year will be because of accidents, so be careful. Try, too, to avoid unnecessary tension and arguments with other people. Take extra care when you are on the roads: no drinking and driving, for example. You will only have problems if you play your own worst enemy. Be extra careful when in the kitchen or bathroom: sharp instruments that you find in these areas can lead to cuts, unless you take care.

Your Sun Sign Partner

Aquarius Woman with Aquarius Man

These two are best friends, soulmates and ideal companions. They're both busier than four people put together, yet they still have time for those late-night talks that cover all topics in the universe in three hours. They love to trade ideas, theories, speculations and curiosities about everything from politics to their best friend's eating habits.

They share the same needs, desires, devotions and attitudes, and when nobody else wants to listen, they know they always have an eager sounding board standing in the wings.

Aquarius Woman

Aquarius woman with Aries man

She impresses him with her humanitarian idealism, and he overpowers her with his list of achievements. She's the kind of woman he loves to talk to, and he is the kind of man to whom she likes to listen.

Beyond this, the basic difference is that he is a taker while she is a giver. He is absorbed by self-interest, she has an interest in every person who crosses her path.

With him, the chances are that she'll end up giving far more than she's getting. She's so good natured that she has a bad habit of sacrificing her own inclinations to other people's strong desires.

However, if he can manage to give her the benefit of the doubt, the two of you could have a fantastic thing going. She'll give him the most extraordinary ideas for his new projects. She won't complain when he works so hard that he rarely sees her. And if he has a little affair here and there – which, in a moment of gut-wrenching guilt, he has to confess – she'll tell him, with a detached smile, not to trouble himself.

Aquarius woman with Taurus man

Any way you look at it, these two are from different planets. He eats different things, he sees different things, and he wants different things. Any interaction will probably be only in passing. If they try to make more of it, frustration could approach the level of paralysis.

He likes to hoard his money and she like to give hers away. She gets carried away by causes; his favourite cause is personal gain. He's enslaved by the material, but her needs are more ethereal.

The communication gap between these two is like a cosmic crack in the universe. If he hangs around her too long, he may fall in.

Aquarius woman with Gemini man

He'll never meet a woman who is as easy to get along with. And she'll never meet a man who is quite as crazy.

≈

She'll love the way he makes her laugh until her sides split. However, she won't appreciate the fact that he is always late and sometimes doesn't show up at all.

Her secret is that, although she is good-natured and will go along with a lot of insanity, she still has feelings. And although she won't mention it, being stood up is not her favourite way of spending an evening.

He'll respect the way her mind works and the fact that it operates in so many directions. And it's not unlikely that she'll capture some place in his heart that he never even knew he had. Mr Gemini may stay up all night trying to figure out what's really happening to him, and why. However, if he just allows himself to forget both time and reason, he'll figure out in the end that it's not really the 'why' that matters.

Aquarius woman with Cancer man

He wants closeness, but she feels more comfortable with distance. He prefers cozy evenings while she embraces crowded situations. He needs a woman who will nurture his strength and overlook his insecurities. She needs a man who has fewer insecurities and a great deal more emotional detachment. She'll become impatient with his super-sensitivity, his mood swings and his possessiveness. At the same time, he'll feel morose and sulky when she gives some meaningless stranger as much as attention as she does him.

Since she is adaptable to most personalities, she could also come to love his. However, if he drowns her in a swamp of emotion and makes too many demands too soon, she'll leave him to his sentimental dreams and memories of an affair that never really was.

≈

Aquarius woman with Leo man

If he marries her, he'll have his own private social worker, physiotherapist and recreational director. But that's only if he ever gets to see her.

The chances are, she knows more people than a politician – and they occupy a special place in her heart. When it comes to people, she has an insatiable attention span and a penchant for helping the problem soul. The phone probably rings till dawn and the doorbell till midnight. At 10 o'clock he'll find her lavishing warmth on the lovelorn, at 2 a.m. she deserts him to aid a 'friend' just gaoled for inciting a protest riot in a clinic. Sometimes he feels he's sleeping in a social welfare unit. At such moments he yells, frowns and grumbles a lot, and sometimes kicks the sofa.

Despite her outward friendliness, she is frightened of human proximity: she is at once loving and kind, freedom-loving and impersonal. He shouldn't try to figure her out; he should just experience her.

Aquarius woman with Virgo man

When he looks at her life, he feels he should take care of her. However, the hardest part comes in trying to convince her that she needs someone. She is a free spirit who feels claustrophobic when anyone gets too close. He's an orderly, controlling type who means well, but may not always have the best ideas. He may love her mind but resent her detachment. He'll get cross when she forgets to do the dishes (even though there's only one fork). However, when she wakes him up in the middle of the night with a theory on the movement of the planets, he'll sit up in bed and give her his full attention.

He has a way of taking up her space with his expectations, making it seem cluttered and confining. On the other hand,

≈

she has a way of making him feel like a spare sock that has less than an even chance of finding its mate. The first thing she needs is freedom. Since this is not something she'll find forthcoming from Mr Virgo, it might be best to look elsewhere and to keep this relationship one of merely friendship.

Aquarius woman with Libra man

She will understand his ego needs and listen to all his problems (even with other women). He's never had such a degree of undivided attention, and naturally it can be habit-forming.

She doesn't make bells ring, lights go on or candles go out, however she does make him feel like he's never felt before. It's a lot deeper than starry eyes; it's more like a devastation.

She will bring him to lectures on meditation and numerology, while he will teach her how to play the guitar. And because she has a million interests and knows a million people, he'll rarely see her, or never have a chance to get sick of her, and will remain sufficiently insecure to maintain a consuming interest.

Aquarius woman with Scorpio man

He'll want to make love, but she'll want to go to the cinema. When he is making love, she'll be musing on why the film ended without music.

He'd better forget trying to control her; she's so detached that she'll end up controlling him. She has about 5,000 friends and takes on the personal problems of each one of them. Therefore, he feels like he's competing with a crowd on opening night.

If he's unfaithful, she'll be too involved with other people's lives to notice. Living with her is like having a roommate. Marriage, to her, is like having a lifelong friend. He'll

≈

never get tired of her, because he'll seldom see her – she's so busy living everybody else's life.

Aquarius woman with Sagittarius man

This is a compatible combination that can provide some exciting moments. He will be rivetted by her many interests, while she will enjoy his overwhelming enthusiasm. They're both freedom-loving, easy-going, fun-loving and adventurous.

He will teach her to ski, while she will teach him meditation. He'll keep her blood churning on the tennis courts, she'll make his mind marvel at all her progressive projects.

They can take each other to a multitude of places, and heartily enjoy themselves along the way. She makes him feel he has a best friend as well as a lover, a most unconventional travelling companion as well as a deeply caring woman.

Aquarius woman with Capricorn man

She is quite eccentric and very freedom-loving, while he is insecure. This is where the differences begin – where they end is an infinity away.

She is a dreamer, he is a materialist. She's fascinated by a multitude of people, but he is more concerned with himself. She's a woman who lives in the future, but Mr Capricorn is consumed by matters close at hand.

They come from different places and are wilful enough to try to bring the other along. Well, it won't work. Therefore, they must learn to accept each other, or both take a walk and look for someone else.

Aquarius woman with Pisces man

She lives in the future, he often gets stuck in the past. She is friendly, yet detached, but he is aloof and sentimental.

She scatters her feelings among many people, while Mr Pisces nurtures his in private places. Basically, the two of them are so different that they seem to be travelling in separate directions. She needs change and constant activity, whereas he is content with the status quo.

She is about as romantic as a cheerful dentist extracting a wisdom tooth; he is intensely sentimental and sometimes a little weak. She has no patience with his armchair observations, and he has no tolerance for her perpetual curiosity. Any relationship closer than backgammon partners is bound to result in mutual irritation.

Aquarius Man

Aquarius man with Aries woman

He is the ultimate challenge, and she hates to admit that he's got her. She thinks he has a beautiful mind, while he thinks she has a beautiful body. She feels she can't get enough of him, but unfortunately he isn't caught up in the same kind of emotion.

He likes women, men, dogs, cats. He's not a snob; he'll speak to anybody. Naturally this bothers Ms Aries, since she wants to overwhelm him to the point that he'll beg to follow her anywhere. However, in this instance she's the one doing the following, and without planning it, he's the leader.

However, this is why he stimulates her; she's always caught between a blizzard and a set of questions and answers. If she can manage her out-of-control feelings, this could be an exciting and rewarding love match. But if she feels that his friendliness causes more pain than she's willing to confront, then it's better that she just be his friend.

≈

Aquarius man with Taurus woman

He is far more interested in what's out in space than in what's right in front of him. And when it comes to those little sensual pleasures that make life worth living, he has a way of reducing them all to thought.

He'll torment her possessive tendencies and put her jealousy through a kind of trial by fire. Communication between the two of them is like a bad telephone connection.

To her mind, he is strange, weird, bizarre and perhaps a little crazy. To his mind, she is confining, conventional, rigid and foolishly wilful.

There's only one thing to do in the face of this meeting: quit while they're still ahead, shake hands, slap each other on the back and come out calling each other 'friend'.

Aquarius man with Gemini woman

She'll stay up all night talking and he'll unfold to her the secrets of the universe. He is always asking 'why', as his personal quest, and never ceases searching – not even in the middle of love-making.

She's intrigued by his genius and by how he seems to make the most simple things complex. He is curious about how she makes the most complex things simple, and thinks her sense of humour is hilarious.

He will share with her his inventions, his universal theories, his friends and his need for freedom. Ms Gemini offers him a superb sense of the ludicrous, and she teaches him how to write down his theories so that he doesn't lose them somewhere in his head.

Although the sexual passion here is not likely to make either of them pass out, the ideas that are mutually inspired are enough to steam up the windows. This could be either a match made in heaven, or a platonic love with the luminescence of the stars.

Aquarius man with Cancer woman

She lives through her emotions, while he relies on his mind. And from this comes the kind of friction that may be more than either of them can handle.

She may think she has to knock him out with a swift karate chop and then hypnotize him with the right words just to get a little romance going. Otherwise, she'll work up the courage to tell him she loves him, and he'll respond that it's really quite fascinating. Just imagine her reaction when he stops and asks her why.

Although he is a good-hearted person, he sometimes gets so entangled in his theories that he reminds her of the mad scientist who sleeps with the test tubes under his pillow. If Ms Cancer wants a man to hug her, make passionate love and remind her how much she means to him, she'd better start looking in another direction.

Aquarius man with Leo woman

He is the detached humanitarian, and she is the emotional narcissus. His desire is to be friends with the world; her desire is to make sure that 'the world' doesn't include other women.

At parties, he thoughtfully observes, while she slinks about to see what he's observing. She just may find that she's spilling her drink over someone else's sleeve when his bright-eyed curiosity keeps him too long in the company of a stunning blonde.

Aquarius is the people-watcher, and Leo is the sign used to being watched. She cannot understand why he can't be content watching her. But from his point of view, another woman's attraction could very well be that she has a split earlobe.

'This man is mad', she's likely to mumble as she turns her back to him to think out a plan of operation. But as she decides to calm down and forgive him, she notices him talking to a gorgeous brunette. She tosses on her coat, twists her lower lip, and crisply informs him that she's leaving.

Aquarius man with Virgo woman

When she tells him her deepest problems, he'll ask her a lot of questions and then offer her a beer. He's far more curious than sympathetic, and somehow it doesn't sit well. She is sensitive, vulnerable and needs someone who will make her feel more secure. He loves her mind, but has no patience with her emotions. It's his opinion that she worries too much. It's hers that he doesn't worry half as much as he should.

Because she takes everybody's feelings to heart, even those of her pet cat, she has a hard time understanding how he can be so detached. At the same time, her obsession with her cat's sinus problems makes him impatient, restless and ready to take a walk. Mentally, there's much stimulation; sexually, there's just a lot of talk. This relationship is best kept on a just-friends level.

Aquarius man with Libra woman

She'll think he's a little strange and eccentric, but also kind and understanding. He hangs out in his head, while she tends to get stuck in her heart.

She'll meet him at a party, where he seems to be talking to everyone at once. He is a people person, and loves to touch as many lives as possible. He comes alive in a crowd, but she prefers an intimate cozy chat. He is detached and warmly impersonal, while she is terribly attached and personalizes everything.

If Ms Libra can discipline herself to enjoy her own company, there need not be a problem. But he needs a woman he feels is an equal in terms of developed individuality.

He'll be her best friend and help her with her problems, but when she starts treating him like a pillow, then suddenly the fun ends. If she can develop the same attitude as his, there are no limits to this relationship. But if she wants a man who is more of a cushion than a thinking being, she's better off avoiding him.

Aquarius man with Scorpio woman

He'll never forget her, because she's an elusive woman. Regardless of the amount of time he spends with her, he'll feel both close and yet far away. However, that is the key to his amorous idealism.

He's extremely opinionated and have at least 5,000 theories on the universe. She should be prepared to hear each one of them. Granted, it may not be the most exciting scenario in which to seduce him. However, if she waits for him to stop talking first, she might as well wait for bronze to turn into silver. It's just not going to happen.

If both of them are open, they could help each other grow and, from this perspective, the relationship has no limits. It will take them as far and as fast as his mind and emotions want to move.

Aquarius man with Sagittarius woman

He'll teach her equations and the history of the world. She'll teach him how to play backgammon and beat him at table tennis.

She'll find him to be one of the most curious and eccentric men she's ever met. When he wears his glasses, he reminds her of Einstein; when they go hiking together, he looks just like the boy next door.

She will be challenged and enchanted by his brilliance; he'll be enamoured of her enthusiasm and philosophic approach to the most trying situations.

Together they can enjoy a future of far-off places. Whether they travel by land or through their minds, a multitude of marvellous will come to them. Every day will be a greater adventure than the day before.

Aquarius man with Capricorn woman

He's a bit more unconventional than she could ever imagine. And more freedom-loving that she may feel comfortable with. However, because he's more fun than a circus, he may make her lose some of her Capricorn control.

She'll faint at his startling intelligence and peculiar ideas. He'll delight her when he shows up at midnight with a bottle of champagne, and the next day sends her roses. Underneath, he is a romantic, though she'd never know it by listening to his theories on the universe.

He is impervious to the considerations of the present, since his mind is like a satellite of the future. On the other hand, Ms Capricorn prefers to live in the here and now, since it depresses her to consider the passage of time.

If she can put up with his physical passivity and decide that she doesn't mind taking total charge of life's menial details, then this could very well become a happy relationship, or even a marriage.

≈

Aquarius man with Pisces woman

Although she respects his intelligence, it wears her nerves a little thin when she's yawning at midnight and he's still babbling on about electron microscopes.

He has absolutely no idea where she's coming from, but he has a wealth of theories. However, each of them, while interesting, somehow misses the mark by a long chalk.

He looks at the world through his mind; Ms Pisces sifts it through her emotions. She's a romantic sentimentalist, while he's a restless man of many interests. He's a humanitarian who feels a lot for everybody in general, but very little for anyone in particular. By contrast, she's an angel of mercy with the kind of emotions that bring the world right into her living room.

As a serious love affair, this probably won't be long-lasting. Both of them are lovable people, but the emotional differences between are enough to drive them apart.

≈

Monthly and Daily Guides

JANUARY

Until 19 January the Sun will be coasting along in the earthy sign of Capricorn, a rather secretive part of your chart. You may be feeling inwardly confident, but for one reason or another you feel unable to be as gregarious and open as you usually are. Maybe something in your private life is bringing you down a bit; however, as an Aquarian, that's not going to be for very long now, is it?

After 20 January the Sun will have moved into the airy sign of Aquarius, your own sign of course, so you'll have approximately three to four weeks when you'll be feeling supremely confident, at ease with yourself but at the same time ready to take on anybody who is out to thwart or irritate you. Mind you, as a kind Aquarian you're not going to be objectionable or too bossy, you'll simply point out that you have a life to lead too, and just for once you cannot run around after other people. Of course this is true.

Mercury, too, will be coasting along in the airy sign of Capricorn up until the 3rd. After this Mercury will be moving into your own sign, making you a little bit restless but full of good ideas and also ready to travel at the drop of a hat. You love to expand in life, don't you – and you are given a couple of weeks for doing just that.

However, it's best to remember that Mercury will be in retrograde movement from 18 January to the end of the month, therefore you must be careful when travelling and on no account put your signature to any kind of contract or paperwork for the time being – well, not until you get the green light from the stars, anyway, otherwise you'll be storing up a lot of unnecessary aggravation and, quite frankly, you don't need it.

From 1 to 18 January Venus is drifting along in Capricorn. This is a signal from the stars to use your instincts when making any kind of decision. There's also a lot going on in the background; make it your business to find out exactly what it is. A warning, however: Venus of course is the planet of love, and because it's in a secretive position there could be a tendency for you to play away from home. Now, Aquarius, you're such an open and honest person normally, you'll never get away with this kind of behaviour, so do try to behave yourself up until the 19th, when Venus will be entering your own sign, making you look good and feel good. You really won't have to do anything to attract others; they're milling around in droves – what a nice position to be in. Furthermore, late in the month is also a good time for anything at all creative, or if you want to form a new partnership.

From 1 to 18 January Mars will be in Pisces, the area of your chart devoted to money. Do take care, because Mars is something of a 'greedy pig'. Not only that, but it will encourage impulsive and headstrong behaviour. If you're going to spend your dosh in this kind of way, you're going to be in a great deal of trouble later on in the year. The choice is entirely up to you.

≈

From the 19th Mars will be moving into Aries for the rest of the month, emphasizing the male friends in your circle, as well as team effort (which could be a little bit tense) and short journeys (in which you could be a little bit impulsive). Minor prangs are a possibility here, but now you've been warned about this, hopefully you're going to do something about it. Remember that Mars will be in Aries from 19 January to 2 March. I know it's expecting a lot for you to behave yourself for such a long period, but at least try to do so, or you'll get yourself into trouble.

The pattern made by the stars, just for once, seems to be placing the emphasis on the other people in your life who hold sway over you in some way, whether your boss, your supervisor, a partner or the family. Just for once you can't be your normal airy-fairy self; you have to consider other people. If you don't do so, you'll be storing up a lot of aggravation and bad feeling. See what you can do.

Finally, Capricorns and fellow-Aquarians are going to be important during this month, so if you're made any kind of offer, even though it may be personal rather than professional, think it over carefully. In this way you will at least be trying to make the most of your particular stars.

1 TUESDAY A decision has been on your mind for long enough. The stars suggest that you can now make a family choice and know that it is the right one. You can speak up for others in a way that gets results. Furthermore, love may feel strained, but whether you know it or not it is working for you, especially if you're single. For some of you, romance can be found while attending some kind of club activity, so stay alert.

2 WEDNESDAY You can't be too careful when it comes to money and friendships. Remember the old adage 'neither a borrower nor a lender be' if you want to remain on friendly terms with other people. This evening could mark the end of a relationship which is perhaps well beyond saving. You'll finally realize that it is time to move on and that is the thing to do.

3 THURSDAY This is a time for playing your own boss and for making your own decisions before other people try to influence your way of thinking. Jog along with the status quo and you will end up doing things for others and not for your-self, thus preventing you from achieving your own goals. I think you'll agree that this isn't right, so make some changes.

4 FRIDAY Today Mercury will be moving into the airy sign of Aquarius, your own sign of course. This will be gingering up your personality, making you long for minor changes, all of which should work out. Paperwork is going to be important, as is keeping on the move from place to place, because while you do so you'll meet interesting people, as well as good chances for getting ahead yourself. Those of you involved in any kind of litigation can relax because you're likely to finish on top, so please don't worry too much, it'll only stress you out.

5 SATURDAY It looks as though events that take place will have you re-thinking ideas and attitudes. This could lead to you making changes in your belief system. The hypocrisy you witness during this particular day does not reflect the views and values of the institution this person claims to represent; it looks as if somebody is being hypocritical.

≈

6 SUNDAY At this moment in time you are far too sensitive to laugh at your worries and woes. If old friends refuse to take your emotional needs at all seriously and take on some of the troubles which should be shared, you should then focus more on a new friend who appears to be more on your wavelength.

7 MONDAY Today Venus and Jupiter line up. These are the 'greedy pigs' of the zodiac, so you will be tempted into spoiling both yourself and those closest to you, and wasting money in general. Well, as an Aquarian you don't see any value in holding on to money unless it's taking you somewhere, and this is especially true on this day, but do double-check the figures on your bank statements before you go stark raving mad.

8 TUESDAY Hard work will bring rewards in various guises. Money will be an incentive, but you will also get the chance to add more experience to your portfolio, standing you in good stead for the future. Grab a new opportunity while this is on offer, because they don't come around too often, I think you'll agree.

9 WEDNESDAY There are benefits to be gained through keeping in touch with people you used to work or study with. The pressure is still on and you need plenty of rest and proper nutrition if you are to keep on top of everything that's going on. Don't promise more than you can comfortably deliver, otherwise you're going to be unpopular.

10 THURSDAY Romance seems to be going through a rather crucial phase; you must take off those rose-coloured glasses of yours and face up to reality in the big wide world. Burying your head in the sand isn't going to make your problems go away; you should know this by now. Therefore, confront difficult issues or you will be faced with an ugly ultimatum, and you won't appreciate it.

11 FRIDAY In order to move forward you must face up to hang-ups from the past and eliminate them completely from your life. You are holding on for dear life to a relationship, situation or belief system which is long past its sell-by date. This is certainly a time for taking control of your life, so see that you do.

12 SATURDAY The stars seem to suggest that a minor hiccough in a technical appliance will be the first of a number of frustrating annoyances and aggravations for you to cope with today. Everything seems to come in threes in this life, but this doesn't apply only to problems but to pleasures, too, so remember that. Therefore, there's plenty for you to look forward to – just believe it.

13 SUNDAY Today is the day of the new Moon, and it occurs in the earthy sign of Capricorn, a rather secretive area of your chart. Your imagination seems to be running rife. Furthermore, you're quite content to work on your own without associating with other people. This could be a good idea, well at least at this moment in time anyway. However, always remember that new Moons are excellent times for making fresh starts for all of us, so choose wisely about which direction in life could benefit from this.

14 MONDAY After some reluctance you accept the need for change by freeing yourself from commitments which are a drain on your time, energy and resources. You are making more space in your life for the people who really mean the most to you. Furthermore, your goals and pursuits are being redefined, and you're putting them in the right order for a change.

15 TUESDAY A professional deal looks to be in danger of collapsing, and your temper is running very short. Do your best to stay as calm as you possibly can. Even if you can't prevent a particular deal from crumbling, look on it as a chance to start anew and to build firmer foundations this time.

16 WEDNESDAY The planetary set-up today suggests that you may be having trouble setting realistic boundaries for yourself. There is every chance you are not seeing the full picture. Until the mist clears you must refrain from making decisions which may take you onto the wrong road. We can't have that.

17 THURSDAY Today's planetary set-up in the stars suggests that you should feel rather touched by somebody else's advances – not to mention a bit self-conscious. You're inclined to think that they must be under some kind of illusion. At any rate, don't be foolish enough to go along with them.

18 FRIDAY Today Mercury goes into retrograde action, therefore you must be careful about signing paperwork, which could be hiding some kind of 'bear trap'. Paperwork and travel may be arduous and should be postponed if at all possible. Lastly, if you have a Virgo or a Gemini in your life, they're going to be a little bit mysterious and difficult to gauge during the next couple of weeks.

≈

19 SATURDAY Although you may now make an impassioned plea, it seems that partners or colleagues already know how desperate you are. Not that they necessarily understand your reasoning powers, even if they are fully aware of your circumstances. But you can be sure that there is no risk of making an idiot of yourself, none whatsoever, therefore this is a time to push ahead.

20 SUNDAY Despite a marvellous link between the planets, other people, especially partners, seem vague or evasive at times. Nevertheless, you still probably envy them because they seem so carefree, while your presence is required elsewhere. Still, if it's any consolation there should be some glad tidings waiting for you once you get home this evening.

21 MONDAY Other people will be persuasive and may tempt you to part with your hard-earned cash on expensive nights out. You should strenuously avoid this. Somewhere beneath that scatty exterior lies a practical heart, and it is time to allow other people to see this and learn to respect it. Do not allow a frivolous mood to break your bank account.

22 TUESDAY Someone's obviously gone to a lot of trouble to accommodate you or fit you into their schedule. You need to ensure that you are well prepared and on time. Admittedly you still can't work out why they asked you along in the first place – but you'll find out once you turn up. In this instance it's true to say that everything happens for a reason.

23 WEDNESDAY On this particular day, things will end on a positive note and you should be more than happy with the way life has progressed. Even so, the link between the planets denotes that you could easily get yourself into a muddle unless you take things one step at a time. Perhaps it would be wise to start planning in advance if you are hoping for a rapid response.

24 THURSDAY The chances are that you have strung someone along – though not intentionally. Now, however, unless you reveal certain facts or information, you could lose out. By doing just that you will not only gain their trust but a lot more besides. In some respects, you'll never have had it so good.

25 FRIDAY You are bound to receive some kind of incentive before today is over and done with. Surprisingly enough, though, this could be a reward for making a long-term commitment, or being a life-line buddy or friend. However, due to some deceptive planetary factors you may have to ward off enquiries about those whom you'd prefer not to mention. Only you know who they are.

26 SATURDAY Today Venus is lining up with Jupiter; because of this you could go well over the top in some way or other. You're feeling confident and great about yourself, and because of this will be only too willing to promise anything to anybody, but remember that the 'crunch time' will come at a later date, and then you'll be feeling and looking perhaps a bit foolish – think twice.

27 SUNDAY The tendency now is to be a bit melodramatic – you seem desperate for attention. Meanwhile, the expression on the faces of partners or loved ones is of amazement, but not because they believe what you are saying is untrue. Any way you look at it, your emotional intensity is quite

≈

frightening. Whether or not they will be predisposed to act remains to be seen.

28 MONDAY This is the day of the full Moon, and it occurs in the fiery sign of Leo, your opposite number. You may find other people feeling either insecure, totally muddled or confused. Whatever you do, don't lecture them. Let them muddle through until they surface on their own. If you do this, they'll be forever grateful to you. As always with full Moons, it's a good time for putting the finishing touches to relationships, to work and anything else you fancy.

29 TUESDAY Your loyalty or staying power is bound to be put to the test today and over the next couple of days. All the same, because of the combined influences of the planets you could become complacent and slow to respond. However, although what is required of you may be time-consuming, there's no doubt it will still come good in the long run, so be patient.

30 WEDNESDAY Long-standing disagreements must be settled if you are to protect your long-term security. It may be a case of coming to your senses and not allowing emotions to influence your judgement. Fortunately you have wise and sympathetic contacts. Professionally this is a most important time, and you now need a great deal of support if you are to succeed.

31 THURSDAY You need to acquire as much information as you possibly can now. At least it is clear that partners, relatives and associates will listen before responding to you. Meanwhile, you have one or two important decisions to make, and will also have found out exactly what everybody is secretly thinking – which you ought to find encouraging. It sounds as if you're being a little bit psychic here.

FEBRUARY

Until 18 February the Sun will be blowing along in the airy sign of Aquarius, your own sign, of course. It is your time of year and you'll have the utmost confidence. You look good and feel good, so you mustn't allow other people to intimidate you. Do what you know to be right, that is the important thing. Never mind the thoughts of other people for the time being.

From the 19th the Sun will be moving into Pisces, the area of your chart devoted to money. What do you know? Just for once you are prepared to save rather than spend – what has come over you? Never mind, we all need a time for conserving, don't we, otherwise our bank managers wouldn't be too pleased, so you're doing the right thing at the right time, and that's always nice to know.

Mercury will be in Capricorn from 4 to 13 February, and you will be able to give free rein to your imagination. This is more of a time for planning than acting, because if you take too much on you will end up feeling drained. On the 14th Mercury moves on into the airy sign of Aquarius; this will liven up your whole personality. It is also possible that you will have news of friends from abroad, and this will lift your spirits.

During the first 12 days of the month Venus will be in your own sign. You look good, you feel good and you're willing to form partnerships and throw yourself into anything which is creative or artistic. Also, romance is definitely in the

≈

air. Should you be fancy-free, someone special may very well enter your life. However, if you already have a mate you're going to have to be careful, because indiscretion is sure to be found out. Bear this in mind.

From 12 February onwards, Venus will be coasting along in Pisces, the area of your chart devoted to money. You could gain from anything creative, or perhaps through forming a partnership. Mind you, you will also feel a strong need to treat yourself and those around, and that can be expensive because you tend to be over-generous. Do try to keep this under control, otherwise you'll find yourself in hot water.

Mars will be coasting along in the fire sign of Aries all month. This could ginger up your thinking, but make you a little bit too impulsive and maybe sharp with other people. If you give in to this, apologies will have to be made at a later date, so see what you can do to control it. Remember, Aries is the sign which denotes short trips; therefore when travelling from place to place take it a bit slowly – what's the rush anyway? If you don't take things easy, there'll be minor prangs which will, later on, prove to be expensive not only in terms of money but perhaps from a legal viewpoint if somebody decides to sue you. Don't go into a panic about this, just be sensible – you usually are, so just proceed in your usual fashion.

The pattern made by the stars places an emphasis on your internal life and what you are thinking. Furthermore, you will be more inclined to spend time at home with your loved ones. They will wonder what on earth has come over you, but we all need a time to build on relationships, and it looks as if this is your chance. Get to know loved ones, particularly children. Sometimes you are a bit of a puzzle to other people, and youngsters can hardly be expected to keep up with you. Just bear this in mind.

≈

1 FRIDAY Any dissatisfaction you're feeling with yourself is now gradually diminishing. Your sense of what you want is becoming less idealistic and more of an everyday challenge. Deep within, instinctively, you know it's the right move to make.

2 SATURDAY Financially you've recently felt in suspended animation. But the stars today are giving you the chance to glimpse what you've been unconsciously ignoring. Suddenly, everything is falling into place, and there's a hint of success on the horizon. Don't neglect your optimistic feelings about how you can gain more. They're spot on.

3 SUNDAY Long-term projects haven't always seemed viable. But the planetary set-up today is bringing you closer to realizing them. Don't make impulsive judgements where others are concerned. Although your ideas are becoming workable, someone might see them all as fantasy. You don't want to be left with an empty dream.

4 MONDAY Today Mercury will be moving into the earthy sign of Capricorn, a rather secretive part of your chart, so you're thinking big thoughts, but quite sensibly not acting for the time being. Give ideas a couple of days to germinate before you leap into action, otherwise you might be sorry. A little bit of time will take you a very long way, I can assure you.

5 TUESDAY Ambivalent feelings have stopped you from enjoying social connections. You're beginning to realize it's because you've been feeling emotionally isolated. But don't delay your desire to get out and about any longer. Somehow all those inhibitions are falling away, and other people are really enjoying your company.

≈

6 WEDNESDAY Cutting loose from others' expectations of you has been difficult. But with the planetary set-up today there's an adventurous influence and you're on the threshold of a new approach to your own aspirations. There's a definite whiff of something positive to come. Proceed with caution until you are really ready to explore any radical dimensions. They're worth waiting for.

7 THURSDAY Things have apparently ground to a halt where your long-term schemes are concerned. You're itching for joint plans to get moving again. The planets' influence finally gives you the chance to redesign and manoeuvre all your plans into a more focused position. But it will take time. Be patient. There are more benefits ahead than you could possibly imagine.

8 FRIDAY Fortunately there's some good news today, and that is the fact that both Mercury and Saturn finally resume direct movement. You no longer have to hesitate about signing paperwork, travelling or mixing with people born under the sign of Capricorn, Virgo or Gemini. Travel will be a good deal easier from now on, and your mind is far more uncluttered than it has been for a while.

9 SATURDAY Getting a relationship right has not been easy over the past few days or so. But with the planetary set-up today you can begin to explore other ways and means of doing so. Of course, it takes two to make it work. But knowledge is one thing, awareness is another. Don't flounder alone. Share your fears and worries and, you never know, that sense of commitment versus independence might not seem so daunting after all, especially as you probably need both to make life complete.

10 SUNDAY It is important that you remember that, no matter how hard life may have knocked you in the past, fear of living restricts you in a harmful way. Past events may have been hard, but now you have learned from them and you will be able to devote more time and attention to those who can fully appreciate your genuine enthusiasm, unconditional love and optimism. Basically you have a good heart, despite what others may have taken from you and regardless of the emotional trials you have undergone. What is best in you is untarnished and pure.

11 MONDAY Questioning whether you can make certain changes in your private life has become almost obsessive for you. But you're beginning to see the light at the end of the tunnel – even though it appears a long way off. You need controlled expansion of your interests. That way you can be sure of making the right choice when the moment comes.

12 TUESDAY Today is the day of the new Moon, and it occurs in the airy sign of Aquarius. This is a good time to put the finishing touches to matters at work, and also to personal affairs – but do take care, because otherwise you might upset others. If you are going out tonight, don't get back too late or things are liable to go sadly wrong.

13 WEDNESDAY Pretending to be one thing when you're actually something quite different may have paid off for a while. But now you have come clean about your true motives and drives. If others can't accept you as you are, don't continue the charade. Your joy for living is more important than resigning yourself to compromises. Start freeing yourself a little.

≈

14 THURSDAY Today Mercury will be moving into your own sign, gingering you up quite considerably, both physically and mentally. Any chances to socialize or travel for the sake of work should be snapped up, and if you happen to have a Gemini in your life, they're certainly going to be giving you the run-around. That's not to say they're being difficult; that's just the way they operate.

15 FRIDAY Typically you have stuck to principles that keep everyone and everything in line on the work front, which has made life easier. But refusing to adapt can bring rigidity. And an idea that's been incubating at the back of your mind is more valid than you thought. Now is the time to let it hatch.

16 SATURDAY What you have been trying to avoid seems to be happening, and the more you try to resist it, the more it seems you're in demand. Romantically, this could be to your benefit. So remember, whatever experiences come your way are simply a reflection of you. Now is the not the time to deny your instincts. Be aware of them.

17 SUNDAY You're caught between the devil and the deep blue sea regarding family and friends. Yet you're beginning to see how both have inhibited your personal freedom of late. It is coming to light that you can begin to speak more openly about your ideas without causing offence. Give yourself the space you deserve; it's time to stop hiding behind a passive mask.

18 MONDAY The planetary set-up today indicates some kind of liaison with someone you are totally captivated by, or have always been attracted to. It's time that you met, even if it is only on a formal basis. You will do so once they are available.

≈

In some ways this is like a second coming – make of that what you will.

19 TUESDAY Today the Sun will be moving into the watery sign of Pisces, the area of your chart devoted to money. This can be no bad thing, because just for once you'll be prepared to conserve and save over the next couple of days, rather than spending too freely. If you want a time for visiting your bank manager, or accountant, this is it; the news will be good and not as you feared.

20 WEDNESDAY Although other people are not very likable and their lack of spirit is extraordinary, you still don't take it personally. You are lucky that you don't have to associate with them, or have a different set-up – or you will very soon. Somewhere, someone will give you an escape route; you might not even have time to say goodbye.

21 THURSDAY You may concede you have missed a great opportunity – and you could kick yourself. But on saying that, it seems that others are still open to offers. Obviously a lot depends on what is left over. You must wait until you've received a proposal and, who knows, you might end up more comfortably off than you thought.

22 FRIDAY You are usually quite shrewd and rather tough when it comes to business. You may decide to keep what you have rather than invest in something which could be a costly mistake – or the best deal you ever made. In this instance you might have to relent for the sake of the family, otherwise you'd not be able to live with yourself. Well, you've always had a conscience, haven't you?

≈

23 SATURDAY A beneficial link between the stars means you should find it easy to reinforce your opinion today – and without anyone over-reacting. In truth, someone rarely says more than a few words and you may not be aware of what they are trying to tell you. They might act without consulting you. Things should prove interesting, to put it mildly.

24 SUNDAY At least certain people can't accuse you of not being totally loyal. Far from it. But it may rankle you that they think you are worth so little. In a way, it is your fault for putting up with the situation and letting them get away with it. However, what materializes right now suggests that your life is about to be greatly enriched and enhanced.

25 MONDAY Like most Aquarians, you tend to take your responsibilities, or duties, fairly seriously – and never more so than at this moment in time. But what you discover now has to ease your mind considerably. You may even be prompted to take a gamble, knowing just how much you could lose. But deep down you know what you are doing is the right thing.

26 TUESDAY A partner, or another person, has been meaning to tell you something, but they haven't considered it that important. Of course, on the surface you will probably remain at your most dignified, but inwardly you are bound to feel hollow. Especially as this concerns someone you have been very upset with.

27 WEDNESDAY The chances are that loved ones, or close companions, have refused to give you any explanation for their behaviour. So no wonder you are upset. Still, you could be in for a surprise, and at least they won't seem quite so closed off now. If anything you should be rather rivetted by what they have to say to you.

28 THURSDAY You are inclined to be forgetful, or are supposed to be anyway. Don't play the scatterbrain right now, because if you do it's unlikely you will have retained certain facts or information which came to light just the other day. It's quite possible that you will be contacted again over the next couple of days, and on this occasion you should express a lot more interest.

MARCH

Until 20 March the Sun this month will be drifting along in the water sign of Pisces, the area of your chart devoted to money, possessions and the materialistic side of life. It's quite possible that you will become more canny than is usually the case at this time, and could pull off a coup or buy something at a bargain price, so keep your eyes peeled.

After 20 March the Sun will be coasting through Aries, the area of your chart devoted to short journeys, the law, certain relatives and the mind. You'll find it easier to concentrate all of your efforts in the right direction, and this will help you to speed your progress in any area that you choose.

Mercury will be in your own sign of Aquarius for the first 11 days of March. You'll be anxious to keep on the move, meet as many new people as possible and, if you have legal matters pending, you can be quite sure that everything will come out in your favour. Mercurial people such as Virgos or Geminis could be extremely useful.

After 11 March Mercury will be moving into Pisces, the financial area of life, and will remain there until the 29th.

≈

There's a strong possibility that you will be travelling on business, signing an important contract and meeting a lot of new faces who will be useful to you, so that can't be a bad thing. Keep alert to the many chances around you, otherwise you'll regret it at a later date.

Venus will be in Pisces during the first seven days of the month. This is the area of your chart devoted to money, so it looks as if you'll be gaining through partnership, or perhaps from something creative.

On 8 March Venus will be moving on into Aries, signalling a time of casual romance. There'll also be plenty of chances for you to have fun. You need a period for letting off steam, and it looks as if it has arrived. Make the most of it because, if you don't, at a later date you will regret it. This is a time for replenishing and refuelling.

Mars will be coasting along in Taurus from 2 March, in the area of your chart devoted to home, family and property. There is likely to be a certain amount of tension and perhaps explosions and bad feelings surrounding these issues. Somebody's got to talk common sense into other people, and you are just the person for doing so – see that you do.

The pattern made by the stars shows that this month is one for self-interest. That doesn't mean you've got to be selfish, just keep an eye open for the main chance and, when it opens up, leap in there and make the most of it. If you don't, you'll regret it for quite some time to come, I can tell you.

1 FRIDAY Today you begin a few days when you're given the green light by the stars to push ahead with everything and everyone that is important to you. There are many times when others may think you're being selfish, but you must carry on regardless of their criticism because, if you allow yourself to be deflected in any way, you may miss out on the chance to do yourself a bit of good, and will be kicking yourself for the rest of the year.

2 SATURDAY Today Mars will be moving into Taurus, where it will stay until the 30th. This is the area of your chart devoted to home and family, and there might be a certain amount of tension and aggravation going on there. Try to keep calm; let others air their differences and then try to make realistic compromises. In that way everybody should be happy.

3 SUNDAY At the best of times you tend to have a head which operates like a grasshopper, leaping from project to project, scene to scene, so if you're to accomplish anything today you'll need to be more focused and disciplined – not easy, but it is either that or a case of rushing around getting absolutely nowhere fast.

4 MONDAY Today is a time when you'll need to double-check anything connected with your social life, romance or affairs related to children, where situations will be changing by the hour. Luckily, you are an adaptable and versatile person, so you should be able to cope. One thing's for certain, Aquarius, you're not going to be bored, and in fact you're likely to revel in everything that's going on. Romance has an exciting feel about it too.

5 TUESDAY You'll be experiencing some wonderful sudden inspirations, though you may find it hard to sit down quietly and do anything practical about them. The best thing to do would be to jot down your ideas so that you can attend to them at a later date when a more practical mood descends. In the mean time, go wherever the wind blows you, because there's one thing for sure right now: you're certainly not going to be bored or boring.

6 WEDNESDAY You're a little bit preoccupied and dreamy today, so you'll need to double-check all of your work – and arrangements – in order to avoid making any kind of mistake. It's important that you get out and about this evening, because friends, neighbours and acquaintances will introduce you to fascinating people. This will either benefit you on the career front, or lead to a new infatuation.

7 THURSDAY The stars suggest you could gain from a calculated risk you took some time ago. It's also a time when you'll be inventing little excuses to celebrate, and this, in turn, could get you a good deal closer to a special person in your life, or, if you happen to be single, bring chances for you to meet new people. One thing's for sure: this day isn't going to be a boring one.

8 FRIDAY It's an ideal time for asking favours from workmates and friends. As an airy Aquarius, you usually prefer to go your own sweet way and be independent, but you must remember that we all need somebody else from time to time, and this is one of those occasions. Make the most of it instead of grumbling.

9 SATURDAY You'll find that your friends and perhaps team mates, too, are positively inspired and, although you may be suffering from feelings of envy (and in extreme cases, jealousy), instead of giving in to these negative emotions, pat your colleagues on the back and offer as much encouragement as

≈

you can, because in doing so you should be able to benefit in some way in the future. It's likely to be a hectic day on the career front, no matter what your job may be.

10 SUNDAY This is a time when you will find yourself in an ideal position for making an important decision, perhaps connected with the family or property matters. If you're single, you'll be drawn to the more gentle members of the human race for a change, so make sure that you're not too boisterous or enthusiastic – you could frighten away a potential admirer.

11 MONDAY The planets will certainly be gingering up matters connected with creativity, children, pleasure and romance. Sports are well starred, whether you are involved with them in your spare time or in a professional capacity. You're certainly likely to be on the winning side and gleaning a great deal in the way of admiration.

12 TUESDAY Today Mercury will be moving into the watery sign of Pisces, the area of your chart devoted to the materialistic side to life. You could be gaining by taking on board a short journey, or perhaps through legal matters which have been hanging fire for a while. Virgos and Geminis will be important for the next couple of days, so listen to what they've got to say.

13 WEDNESDAY This is an ideal time for bringing a set of circumstances and a relationship to a grinding halt. On the other hand, if you value someone who is close to you and the relationship is going through a rocky phase, you'll need to pull out all the stops and turn on the charm if you are to rescue what the two of you have.

≈

14 THURSDAY Today is the day of the new Moon, and it occurs in the watery sign of Pisces, the area of your chart devoted to money. There could be a fresh source of income in the pipeline. Be alert to all opportunities to swell that bank balance, because they don't come along too often and you really need this. New Moons are always a good time for making any kind of fresh start.

15 FRIDAY Today the stars put you in an aggressive, impulsive and perhaps bad-tempered mood. If you are feeling at all stressed, set aside some time for relaxation, periods during which you can let the whole world drift away, because in this way you'll be replenishing, refuelling and making ready to enjoy yourself this evening. Slow down as you rush from place to place because minor mishaps are a possibility.

16 SATURDAY There are times when other people tend to think of you as something of a scatterbrain, but you know, Aquarius, you can be just as grounded and as imaginative as the next person, as you are about to prove to all and sundry right now. This evening looks promising from a romantic viewpoint, so if you are unattached do make sure that you're looking your best and circulating as much as possible.

17 SUNDAY The stars suggest you are dwelling in the past, and perhaps on someone special you met earlier in the year, even though you know there's no point dreaming about what might have been. This is a time for living in the present and taking it on, perhaps in the way of solving problems or laying down plans for the future.

≈

18 MONDAY You are provided with an excellent 24 hours for chasing money owed you. This is a great time for finding bargains, because when it comes to negotiating you are unbeatable right now. You're almost certain to be richer by the end of the day, if not in pocket then most certainly in experience or wisdom.

19 TUESDAY You may find progress on the work front blocked at every turn. Mind you, a lot of these obstacles lay between your ears rather than in reality, so see what you can do to unclutter your busy head and face life as it really is, not how you believe it to be. In doing so you'll make the day a good deal more pleasant and straightforward.

20 WEDNESDAY If you're a parent, teacher or in some way responsible for younger people, you'll find it relatively easier today to sort out a muddle in connection with children. For other Aquarians, make certain that you're looking your best at all times, because romance seems to be knocking at your door. Lucky you – make sure you are ready to take advantage of this fact.

21 THURSDAY Today is the day when the Sun will be moving into the fiery sign of Aries, the area of your chart devoted to the affairs of brothers and sisters, short-distance travel and the mind, which is firing on all cylinders. The next couple of days or so you'll have faith and confidence in your thoughts, put them into operation, and be glad you did.

22 FRIDAY It's likely that you'll be meeting many new people today. Some will be useful in helping you to achieve your ambitions, while others will turn into good friends who will be helping you to make the most of your social life. An especially good day for team effort.

23 SATURDAY Your mind is busily working and your body wants to travel. There could be a bit of a conflict here. Mind you, you'll be given plenty of chances to show other people how creative you really are and, on a romantic level, there's an above-average chance of you running into a brief encounter which may, or may not, develop into something more. The outcome is, as always, dependent on you.

24 SUNDAY The stars suggest that you should be a little wary when out shopping, because you'll be prone to mad extravagances which you can ill afford for the time being. Mind you, you're provided with an excellent day for meetings with people connected with cash, so if you're professionally involved with a friend, a neighbour or even a relative, you can sit down and plan what the next move should be.

25 MONDAY The stars suggest that you are happy to root around in the background of things, perhaps in an effort to uncover a truth or maybe search for the answer to a financial problem. Either way, you're going to be much more serene and preoccupied than usual. Those who know you well will decide you're coming down with some kind of illness, because a quiet Aquarian is a very rare thing indeed. Never mind, you always do have that special ability to surprise the rest of us.

26 TUESDAY There's an indication today that you could be falling in love, or at the very least be wildly infatuated, depending on your age, of course. There's a happy feel about your social life, too, so get out your best outfit, get out into the world and give it a good shaking.

27 WEDNESDAY You're provided with a day for making changes, particularly where cash matters are concerned. If you've any ideas, don't be slow to come forward. Other people will be hanging on your every word, because it's you who is likely to be in the limelight at this time. Don't waste this opportunity. Make sure you keep in circulation this evening.

28 THURSDAY Today is the day of the full Moon, and it occurs in the airy sign of Libra, the area of your chart devoted to matters related to higher education, legal affairs and far-off places, all of which could be a little bit stressful or difficult. Instead, why don't you use the full Moon for putting the finishing touches to those many jobs and projects you have lying around? That way, you'll be using the day productively.

29 FRIDAY There's a lively feel about the day, so make sure you take advantage of energetic prevailing conditions at this time. It's a particularly good day for making new friends and contacts, especially if you believe they can help you in connection with your ambitions.

30 SATURDAY Others will be splashing out buying a much-longed for possession and deriving a great deal of pleasure from it. You may feel a little bit envious, but you really can't afford to do the same. Mind you, it's the best possible time for making important changes and decisions, especially if they are connected with the monetary side of life.

≈

31 SUNDAY You're at your most scatty and disorganized today, therefore double-check your diary and make sure you know where you're supposed to be and at what time, otherwise people could be in for a disappointment, and one of them might be you. Not the best possible day for signing contracts. You'll need to get them checked out first, or you'll live to regret it.

APRIL

Until 19 April the Sun will be coasting along in the fiery sign of Aries, the area of your chart devoted to short-distance travel, casual relationships and the mind, which seems to be full and imaginative.

On 20 April the Sun will be moving along into Taurus, the area of your chart devoted to home, family and property affairs, all of which will take precedence over anything else. Furthermore, it's likely you'll be entertaining at home more than you usually do, and enjoying the experience immensely, as will your guests.

Mercury stays in Aries until 12 April, so your mind is firing on all cylinders. A good time for short-distance travel, presenting ideas to other people and, of course, legal affairs, in which you can hardly go wrong unless you really try – see that you don't.

Mercury will be in Taurus from the 13th. This is a time for opening new lines of communication and also for entertaining at home. If there has been a difficult situation bubbling under the surface recently, you should now bring it out into the open and sort it out.

Venus is in Taurus from 2 to 25 April, again the area of your chart devoted to home and family. Obviously the stars

≈

are trying to tell you something. Maybe you're neglecting those at home, or perhaps being a little bit brisk with them. Try to be as affectionate as you can, and try to find out what they're thinking about. If you do this, you'll not only draw a lot closer to them, but will be creating the harmony that you invariably seek.

Mars will also be in Taurus until 13 April, so unless you take the advice given above, tension, arguments and stresses will be building. Somebody's got to see common sense, and with your logic, Aquarius, it might just as well be you. It doesn't look as if anybody else is going to. Don't crow about your superiority, just be quietly confident. On the 14th Mars moves on into the airy sign of Gemini. Oh dear! There could be bad feelings in connection with almost anything to do with social or artistic life.

The pattern made by the stars suggests you should be thinking of other people rather than yourself. Others will certainly be reaching out to you, both romantically and on a business level. It's up to you to recognize this as quickly as you can. Sometimes Aquarians can be drifting on their own astral plain and are not really aware of what's going on, but behaving this way during April could mean that you will lose out, and that would be a great pity.

1 MONDAY You seem to be on the way to greater self-fulfilment, and the stars today assure that there is no better time for finding the bright lights you seek. Stimulating companions and changes of scene set the tone at this time. We all need help to make our own luck, so there's no reason for staying stuck in a well-worn rut. Look for a diversion.

≈

2 TUESDAY Today you seem to be warming up, being much more proud, open-minded and perhaps a little 'showy'. Certainly during this time the way to your heart is going to be through softly spoken flattery, which you'll fall for every time. So you'd better take care in your emotional life, otherwise you could get hurt.

3 WEDNESDAY Life is, of course, full of contradictions, and this day highlights an important mental change. Recently you have decided to make the best of a personal situation that in the past has led you to imagine that the grass was greener somewhere else. Having come to terms with reality, you're now experiencing a surprising increase in vitality and enthusiasm. Life is throwing you a wild card which you should play to the fullest extent, both romantically and professionally.

4 THURSDAY An unexpected alteration to your working life makes it necessary for you to re-think the whole nature of what you're trying to achieve. Unexpected developments could turn out to be a blessing, cashwise, but there is a great deal that seems to be still in the air. You need to play for time before feeling able to make decisions in connection with long-term commitments. It's important to extricate yourself from minor details so you can see the larger picture.

5 FRIDAY People will be ridiculously optimistic and enthusiastic and, although you may find their mood infectious, don't get completely carried away, otherwise you could all make a gigantic mistake. Certainly this evening, individuals should take whatever you say with a great mountain of salt; your flattery is about as insincere as it's possible to be.

≈

6 SATURDAY Beware of taking liberties where officials or bureaucrats are concerned, because you most certainly won't get away with it. You may be feeling a little 'flat' this evening, so the best thing to do is not to sit around brooding, but to get on the phone and get together with somebody who can bring a smile to your face.

7 SUNDAY You're certainly taking a much more serious attitude towards your emotional life. Many of you may even be prepared to make a commitment at this time. Providing you have thought things through for a sufficient amount of time, there's no reason why you shouldn't do so. Older people will be passing on some good advice – make sure you're listening.

8 MONDAY Today you could be incredibly impatient and aggressive, and concentration flies out the window. Best then to occupy yourself with routine work that you can do blindfolded, because if you take on any new challenges you'll be getting hot under the collar and will probably be at your least efficient. Make sure you control a tendency to criticize others this evening, or somebody will be hurt.

9 TUESDAY You want to fly high, but what has happened recently has given you more than your fair share of ups and downs. Still, rest assured that you have everything you need to take off again, even if life does seem changeable. Make sure you read the situation correctly before trying to make your mark. Timing is as important as what you're trying to achieve.

10 WEDNESDAY While you stay closely tied in with others, your finances will be prone to circumstances that are perhaps beyond your control. The stars may find you thinking over a problem, perhaps in connection with your status, but no amount of bargaining or wheeling and dealing can influence your situation. Try to be independent and spend time accepting your talents and working on your weak spots. Others may be indecisive, but you get on with your life.

11 THURSDAY You're feeling positive today, and in your current creative frame of mind you can conquer your doubts and triumph over the fear of being led up the garden path by someone who claims to have your best interests at heart. It might seem that all the attention is on other people, but don't worry about feeling left out, what you should be doing is trying to find out what's going on in someone's mind.

12 FRIDAY Today is the day of the new Moon, and it occurs in the fiery sign of Aries, the area of your chart devoted to short-distance travel, the mind (which will be a good deal clearer than it usually is) and the affairs of brothers and sisters. As always with new Moons, it's a good time for making a fresh start, so don't let the grass grow under your feet.

13 SATURDAY You have a great day for making important decisions, for clearing the clutter from your brain and deciding exactly what your next move should be. Don't be afraid to discuss problems with someone more experienced than yourself; those who have been in your current position before will help you to decide exactly what you should do.

14 SUNDAY Today Mars will be moving into the airy sign of Gemini, the area of your chart devoted to creativity, sport, children and casual romance. Where physical activity is concerned, do take things easy otherwise you'll be prone to

≈

strains, sprains and impatience. Calm down, take things a step at a time and you really won't go wrong.

15 MONDAY This is not a time to take liberties with rules, regulations or the law; if you do, this could prove costly. Use your common sense, Aquarius – hunt around and see if you can dredge it up. Possibly it's hiding in a cupboard some-where, so have a good clear out.

16 TUESDAY The stars increase your imagination and are drawing you to everything which is colourful, sensitive and perhaps creative, too. This evening you should choose your company carefully and spend your time with people who are sympathetic and gentle, those who are more ready to give you some advice if you believe you need it. If you are out dating, don't get too carried away on a fluffy pink cloud; keep one little toe on terra firma.

17 WEDNESDAY You could become more easily upset than is usually the case, especially where minor difficulties are con-cerned. This could make you more than usually critical. There will be occasions today when you could be quite unreason-able, but hopefully, now that you are aware of the fact, you'll recognize them and side-step any pitfalls. You're also provided with an excellent time for signing on the dotted line where property matters are concerned.

18 THURSDAY You're spending time thinking about where you need to put yourself in order to establish some solid roots. So many different ideas captivate your imagination, and you're perhaps clouding the main issue: where can you feel free to be yourself without having to fit in with somebody

≈

else's ideas? Well, Aquarius, there are times when your nerves run ragged to the point of needing to be more private. Find some sort of sanctuary and replenish yourself today.

19 FRIDAY You seem to be suffering from a certain lack of direction when it comes to putting ideas into practice. Although you know you want to push out into life, uncertainty seems to be putting you on hold. Sitting around doing nothing is not your idea of fun, but perhaps you ought to consider progressing with two steps forward and one step back. After all, this is some kind of progress.

20 SATURDAY Today the Sun will be moving into the earthy sign of Taurus, the area of your chart devoted to home, family and property. You'll be doing a lot more entertaining on your home base from here on in and will be enjoying the experience too, as indeed will be your loved one. So go for it.

21 SUNDAY A coolness or a change of heart by somebody else may have jogged you out of spending all your time worrying about the material side of life, and perhaps made you realize just how much emotional security means, although you very rarely admit it. This could be just the time for letting your defences down, because the current situation seems to suggest that you might be better off without them.

22 MONDAY You may be feeling rather vulnerable today, but at least you realize exactly who your friends are, and also understand that others often have hidden motives that don't come to light unless you scratch the surface. Valuing yourself brings more esteem from others. Don't underplay your own view of life and determination to live it as an individual.

≈

23 TUESDAY The stars may be raising doubts within you, or perhaps due to someone else's lack of commitment. You've often found it easy to slide away from people or situations that make you feel unsure, but right now the stars offer you the chance to try another tack and face problems full-on. Be honest with yourself and face your current needs, rather than drifting with the tide.

24 WEDNESDAY Your brain cells will be hopping around like crazy today. If your job relies on originality, you're certainly going to be doing well for yourself over the next couple of days or so. Today, though, it might be a good idea to find company locally; there are plenty of chances for having fun in this way, and you're really not in the mood for being too adventurous.

25 THURSDAY A tough time seems to be in store for those of you who work in offices. On the other hand, if you are a salesperson, visiting clients, you're sure to have the gift of the gab and will be at your most persuasive, and because of this order books are likely to be full. This evening, brief encounters prove to be exciting and fun, but shouldn't be taken too seriously.

26 FRIDAY There seems to be a great deal of movement going on at home right now. This seems to suggest that you may either have visitors 'sleeping over', or the house may be full of smiling faces this evening. Certainly a good time for home entertaining, anyway.

27 SATURDAY Today is the day of the full Moon and it occurs in the watery sign of Scorpio, the area of your chart devoted to work. It's a good idea to put the finishing touches

≈

to jobs that you've left hanging around for a very long time. If you don't, somebody will find out and you will appear to be inefficient – and that would hurt a great deal.

28 SUNDAY It's likely that you'll feel the need to spend money on your home. In some instances this may be due to the fact that something has finally broken down and needs replacing. For others, you might simply want to spruce up your home, because possibly you want to make a big impression on a potential partner.

29 MONDAY Among other things, fun and sport seem to be well starred, so if you work in entertainment, leisure time activities, or even with children, you can expect a couple of days chock-a-block with activity and news. If not, then your love life will be enhanced. Circumstances seem to be changing within a relationship.

30 TUESDAY It seems that those closest to you are likely to be over-confident about the outcome of a situation. While you may not feel like playing the 'wet blanket', it still might be a good idea to encourage other people to wait and see before they jump to conclusions, because this is the way to disappointment.

MAY

Until 20 May the Sun will be drifting along in the earthy sign of Taurus, the area of your chart devoted to home, family and property affairs. If you need to give any of these sides of life a kick-start, this is the time for doing just that.

On 21 May the Sun will be moving along into Gemini and the area of your chart devoted to long-distance travel, imports/exports, friends related to abroad and further education, so you may be keen to take on a course of learning to improve your mind – this is the right time to do it.

Mercury is situated in Gemini too, so even though you may be sitting at home, people you know in distant lands will be getting in touch with you. Furthermore, it's a great time for sorting out legal matters if absolutely necessary, because 'right' seems to be on your side.

Venus is also in Gemini until 20 May; strange-sounding accents are likely to be 'turning you on' where love and sex are concerned. However, if you already have a mate, for heaven's sake behave yourself because you'll certainly be found out if you don't.

Venus will be in Cancer from 21 May; this suggests a happy time at work. You are relaxed, creative and will be able to mix business with pleasure.

Mars is also in Gemini, therefore it's quite clear that if you have anyone in your circle, or in your family, born under this particular sign, their wants and needs will take precedence over your own. What's more, this sign could be lucky for you, so if you see some stranger waving their arms around and chatting a million miles an hour, you can be quite sure they're born under the sign of the Twins and it might be a good idea for you to make an effort to get to know them better.

All in all, May seems to be full of possibilities – of course, it's entirely up to you to make the most of it.

1 WEDNESDAY Today you can't rely on the promises that come to you through friends, contacts or acquaintances. Certainly they mean well at the time, but circumstances beyond their control may stop them from coming across with what has been promised to you. Nobody is to blame.

2 THURSDAY This is an ideal time for meeting with your bank manager, accountant and people in positions of power or influence. Officials can also be won round by your glib tongue, but don't imagine you can fool them completely – they'll wake up to you at a later date, so don't be cheeky.

3 FRIDAY Concentration is fantastic and you should turn your attention to all those little details which normally you would brush to one side. You may also be receiving some wise advice from a more experienced head this evening – the only question is, are you going to listen? I certainly hope so, because they seem to be talking a good deal of common sense.

4 SATURDAY Any worries you may have had about a loved one's ability to earn a living will slowly begin to disappear, and your faith in them will return. Double-check your arrangements with other people this evening, because the stars could be making them unreliable.

5 SUNDAY You will find that friends, contacts and acquaintances will become more intense and perhaps also more preoccupied with their own affairs, so they have precious little time for you. There's no need to take umbrage about this, after all, you have been a little demanding of late. Now it's time for you to stand on your own two feet – something you do very well when you have to.

6 MONDAY Progress is going to be difficult over the next few days, so every step you take forward will necessitate taking two back. Because you have only a small degree of patience, your temper will be flaring at the slightest provocation.

≈

Remember, the situation is only temporary; this will help you to get through.

7 TUESDAY If you're doing any kind of studying, concentration could break down at any moment. There's no point in getting angry or irritated, just take things at a slower pace and all will be well. Those of you who are travelling any distance today would be well advised to double-check your arrangements, otherwise you'll be left unnecessarily hanging around, and that will only make you cross.

8 WEDNESDAY There's a rosy glow over everyday work which needs to be done; you'll be tackling it at the speed of light and will have time to spare. Last-minute changes may also be made to your social and romantic arrangements, but luckily you're an adaptable soul and you should be able to cope with this quite cheerfully.

9 THURSDAY You have a few days when social life and romance are very much emphasized, and the good times seem to lie ahead for you. This new atmosphere will also be useful for those of you who are professionally involved in the arts, with children, and also with sport. If any of this applies to you, pull out all the stops and go after what and whom you want.

10 FRIDAY The stars are likely to bring a certain amount of movement and news in connection with your friendship circle. However, if someone decides to confide in you, you'd be extremely unwise to betray their confidence because, at a later date, you'll be found out and may lose a treasured relationship, which would be a great pity. However, the ball is in your court; it's up to you how you decide to serve it.

≈

11 SATURDAY You could be in one of your scatty moods, so progress is likely to be stalled because of inefficiency. The best thing to do is to trim down unnecessary work and apply yourself completely to what takes top priority on your list of important issues. Don't allow yourself to be side-tracked by fun-loving colleagues.

12 SUNDAY Today is the day of the new Moon, and it occurs in the earthy sign of Taurus, the area of your chart devoted to home, family and property. There could be a new beginning as a result of this, but don't worry about it; it'll work out well. As always, new Moons are a great time for doing anything special.

13 MONDAY Be very careful of any so-called opportunities to have fun which crop up completely out of the blue. It's likely that they may seem glamorous, but, as usual, you haven't bothered to do your homework. Because of this you'll be disappointed and end up realizing that you've wasted the entire day. Stick to your well-laid plans and you'll be able to avoid this unfortunate state of affairs.

14 TUESDAY Your mood today seems to be one of uncertainty and you could suffer from irrational fears. One side of your brain recognizes this, but the other is prepared to give in to them. Inner battles are likely and, because of this, you need to pace yourself during the day and not place too many heavy demands on your time. It would be a good idea, for example, to get in an early night.

15 WEDNESDAY Today Mercury goes into retrograde movement. Oh dear! It's quite clear that from here on in, until this state of affairs rectifies itself, you should avoid unnecessary travel or flouting the law. Should you have a Virgo or a Gemini in your life, they're going to be rather awkward and you'll need to make allowances – see what you can do.

16 THURSDAY You can push ahead with everything which is important to you, including minor changes. If you're trying to attract the attention of a potential date, this is the time to step up to centre-stage and make sure you are noticed. Mind you, it's very difficult to imagine that anyone could possibly over-look an Aquarius. But, just in case they do, keep a prominent place in all of the activities which are going on around you.

17 FRIDAY Right now others seem to be hell-bent on influ-encing you, but you really must base your choices on your own opinion of what is right for you. The stars are smoothing a path for you which will take you exactly where you want to go, provided you don't allow anyone to side-track you. Once you've weathered a few storms, there will be every reason to believe that you're on a straight run towards great improve-ment in your affairs.

18 SATURDAY The stars provide you with a lighthearted day, one when you need to let off steam in physical activities such as sport, or simply relax in the company of close friends. Romance has a flirtatious feel about it, and you should accept all chances to have fun which come your way at this particu-lar time.

19 SUNDAY The stars suggest you won't have to wait any longer for people to make up their minds. Information or news which comes your way should open up a whole new field of possibilities. However, it's likely that you still need to handle those closest to you with a certain amount of loving care and attention. There's a fair amount of negotiating to be done in connection with a delicate matter, but it seems that you hold most of the trump cards.

20 MONDAY There's a return of optimism and enthusiasm. There's no reason at all to stay stuck, constantly going over old ground, when so much is opening up in other directions. Where relationships are concerned it's likely you'll be quite surprised by somebody else's kindness. Nothing restores your faith in yourself quite so much as unexpected appreciation.

21 TUESDAY Today Venus will be moving into the watery sign of Cancer and the area of your chart devoted to health matters (which should be thriving, just as long as you don't eat or drink too much), work matters (which are also doing well, especially if they happen to concern anything artistic), and partnership affairs of a professional nature. As long as you're prepared to co-operate with others, all should be well. Don't go off on your own.

22 WEDNESDAY The Sun has now moved into the airy sign of Gemini. Once more we have an emphasis on sport, matters related to children, creativity and casual romance. There's a nice lighthearted feel about this period, so do make sure that you make the most of it, otherwise you will regret it later.

23 THURSDAY You like to keep on the go, and today the stars suggest that most of the activity and attention should be centred on home, parental and family affairs. Well, Aquarius, you can't ignore relatives all the time and, if you want to sort out misunderstandings between somebody else and your good self, the stars will go a long way to helping you do so without ruffling anybody's feathers.

24 FRIDAY Money and relationships seem to be somehow connected at this time, and you're having to find a balance between your happy-go-lucky nature and the cash realities of life. However, you do have to be more determined now, and you should resolve to make a clear divide between your ideal version of life and reality. Nevertheless, it is your ability to become inspired by your vision or something greater that ultimately spares you from being limited by boring daily routine.

25 SATURDAY By now you've probably heard all the promises in the book, and are getting a bit fed up with other people spinning tales. Luckily, today the stars will help you to bring endless speculation to a conclusion. Now the choices are laid out so you can choose where to go from here. Your excellent powers of discrimination should make it clear that the only way forward is in the direction of personal happiness.

26 SUNDAY Today is the day of the full Moon; it occurs in the fiery sign of Sagittarius, the area of your chart devoted to friends, team effort and redefining your goals. It's a great time, too, for putting the finishing touches on plans and projects – but perhaps not the time for reaching out too adventurously.

27 MONDAY You can expect a certain amount of confusion to set in. Unusually, you don't seem to know where you want to go or with whom, but if you humour yourself and understand that this is only a temporary hurdle which will soon pass, you'll save yourself a lot of aggravation. In the mean time, use this day for putting finishing touches to jobs around the house, or at work. It might be a good idea to get in an early night.

28 TUESDAY Those closest to you will be impulsive, impatient and even bad-tempered. The ideal way to travel is alone – distance yourself from their wants, needs and suggestions because, really, you are the only person who knows what the best thing for you is at this time. This evening you may be prone to a mad sexual attraction, but don't mistake it for anything more important.

29 WEDNESDAY The stars are testing your ability to get on with others. Even so, it is possible to consider other people too much, to spend too much time trying not to rock the boat. This is hardly the way to live your life; as an air sign you really must do what you want to do. What happens today could bring a new dimension to a relationship that has settled into a pattern. The time has come to surprise even yourself.

30 THURSDAY You may find yourself in a situation where you're experiencing divided loyalties. Amidst all the pushing and tugging, it's simply impossible to please everybody all the time. Even so, you must ensure that you come out of the fight with a clear idea of your own priorities. Believe it or not, you have the opportunity to grasp what is actually most precious to you.

31 FRIDAY Carrying on as you are or risking higher stakes seems to be the issue raised by the planets today. Restricting your options to a choice of two merely increases the pressure and limits your potential. Luckily, the stars will allow you to see many other possibilities. You might value endurance to a

≈

degree, but the stars strongly suggest that you don't sell yourself short at this time.

JUNE

Until 21 June the Sun will be drifting along in the airy sign of Gemini, the area of your chart devoted to matters related to children, creativity, sport, casual romance and good times. So it seems that you have a great deal to look forward to.

On 22 June the Sun will be moving into Cancer, the area of your chart devoted to sheer hard work, health matters and relationships with workmates. If you encounter any hiccoughs at this time, lower your guard just a touch and let other people in – you'll discover that this will work wonders, so why not give it a whirl?

Mercury continues in Gemini all month, making this a good time for signing contracts, especially if they are to do with creative work. You have lots of imaginative ideas, so share them with others – they are bound to be impressed.

On 15 June Mercury will be moving into the fiery sign of Leo – and that, of course, is your opposite number. Other people will be chatty, gossipy, full of bright ideas and ready to listen to you, too. New relationships may spring up. They're not likely to be intense or world-shattering, but they will bring a certain warmth into your life because friendship is very important to you, perhaps more than for most signs.

Venus will be in Cancer for the first 14 days of the month, in the area of your chart devoted to relationships with workmates, which seem to be thriving as each day passes. However, there may be a tendency for you to give in to overindulgence. If so, you'll find yourself on the sick list, so try to avoid this wherever possible.

≈

Mars will be drifting along in Cancer all month, so workmates may become a little bad-tempered, tense and uncooperative during the latter part of the month. There's nothing you can do about this except put your head down and get on with what you've got to do. If other people want to rant and rave, that's their business. You stay well out of it.

The pattern made by the stars suggests that you're being extremely intense about two or three sides of life, and ignoring everything else. Only you know which sides of life these are; perhaps you should try to redress the balance, otherwise you'll regret it and wish that you'd paid more attention to things which, at the time, you thought unimportant, but at a later date turn out to be of major significance.

1 SATURDAY The stars suggest you're not going to get anything for nothing, and there's no point in even thinking you will. It's very much a time for putting your nose to the grindstone and clearing up a backlog of work, so that you are unfettered, uncluttered and, therefore, more able to decide what your next move should be. This evening you may decide to socialize with a workmate. There's no reason why you shouldn't, just as long as you're not hoping to mix business with romance.

2 SUNDAY Your opposite number, whether it be at work or at home, seems to be in a romantic frame of mind and also rather frisky. If you want to criticize them in any way, shape or form, make sure you couch your words with sweetness and light – although, of course, it wouldn't be a good idea to overdo this. All that really matters today is that you open a door which has been tempting you for quite some while, and find out what's on the other side. See that you do.

≈

3 MONDAY Today Uranus will go into retrograde movement. This is your ruling planet, of course, and so from here on in for quite some time you will discover that for every step you take forward it's necessary to take three back. Certainly there may be a break in this tension from time to time – this little book will help you to find out when, as indeed it will inform you when Uranus resumes direct movement.

4 TUESDAY Life should be less fraught with complications and irritations from now on. You feel free to take a trip, sign on the dotted line and generally do everything in your power to propel yourself towards a brighter future. Nobody can hold you back, Aquarius, so take your fate in your own hands and push ahead.

5 WEDNESDAY Other people may be unreliable, so if you have any arrangements with them, for heaven's sake get on the telephone and check that they know exactly where they're supposed to be and at what time, otherwise you'll be left kicking your heels with steam pouring out of your ears. Patience isn't exactly your strong point, particularly today.

6 THURSDAY There's a happy glow over relationships with workmates, and this also makes the daily grind more acceptable. Healthwise, there'll be a tendency for you to be drawn into excesses, and although a little bit of what you fancy may do you good, a lot of the same can put you on the sick list, and that would never do. You're far too impatient and active to waste time in such a way. So promise yourself that you'll keep a sense of proportion and stay as fit as a flea.

≈

7 FRIDAY There's a frustrating feel about this particular day: one moment you're given the green light to push ahead, the next minute you run up against a brick wall and need to slow down. It's enough to drive a true Aquarian round the bend and back again. Still, it's only a 24-hour period and, as long as you take it in your stride, you'll be fine. Get out your adaptability and resilience, because you're most definitely going to need both.

8 SATURDAY Today Mercury finally decides to resume direct movement, therefore there'll be no more problems in connection with paperwork, travel or matters related to foreigners. Furthermore, if you want to sign on the dotted line or take a trip, this is the time for spoiling yourself – and why not?

9 SUNDAY It's likely that you will decide that there is no point waiting patiently for other people to make the first move. If you want something to happen, you must take the initiative yourself. Today the stars convince you that it's high time you spoke up and laid your cards on the table. Certainly there's a strong possibility that you can make at least one of your dreams come true, so push ahead.

10 MONDAY Today is the day of the new Moon and it occurs in the sign of Gemini, the area of your chart devoted to casual romance, creativity, sport and matters related to children. If you need to make changes in any of these areas, then the stars are advising you to push ahead, so see that you do.

11 TUESDAY It's lucky that you're adaptable, because today is likely to bring minor changes to most of your relationships. Be ready for anything. Important news can be expected if you

≈

work in a professional partnership. Don't make hard-and-fast plans or rules today, just allow yourself to be blown along with the wind, as you usually do. This is the most positive approach to life you can take at this time. Those of you waiting for news from abroad should not be disappointed.

12 WEDNESDAY Minor changes at work will, believe it or not, work to your advantage, though it may not seem that way for the moment. Luckily you are an air sign, so it's possible to push you in this direction without even making you blink an eye. Flexibility will certainly be serving you well during this particular day. If you have something of a crush on a workmate, this is not the time for declaring your feelings.

13 THURSDAY If you need to sort out a child, this is the time for sitting them down and trying to make them see sense. If it's romance you're after, there will be plenty of opportunities but it's doubtful that you'll be able to develop a relationship for the time being.

14 FRIDAY You're at your most creative and optimistic, a positive boon to any surroundings you may find yourself in. Having fun is certainly top of your priorities during the evening, and any chances that crop up to paint the town various shades of purple will be snapped up without further ado – who can blame you?

15 SATURDAY Today Venus will be moving into the fiery sign of Leo, your opposite number. There is a happy, contented glow over all of your close relationships, be they professional or personal. It's likely, too, that you may develop something of a passion for someone on the work front, and you may be delighted to discover they feel the same way as you do. How very nice.

16 SUNDAY The stars are helping you discover what you want out of life; this is going to become a good deal clearer to you. You'll be reshuffling your priorities, working out how you can turn a situation to your advantage and coming up with the answer, too. Socially, it would be a good idea to keep on the move this evening, because you've plenty of energy to spare.

17 MONDAY You might be inclined to withdraw from activities that are going on around you, and this is just as well because you need to time to relax. It's possible that you have an important decision to make and, in this respect, you have no intention of being hustled or hassled by other people, and quite right too. Take your time, Aquarius; you don't have to rush around as if the devil were at your heels.

18 TUESDAY There is a tendency for you to give in to excesses where all your appetites are concerned, including sex. But remember, your judgement isn't that great and it would be easy for other people to fool you into believing they are something they are not. Still, as long as you don't go overboard all should be well.

19 WEDNESDAY If you work professionally with children, in the arts or in connection with sport, your social life is going to be more important and hectic than it has been for some time – but you're not going to complain about this, are you? Romantically, nobody should be taking you seriously because you're at your most flirtatious and are simply testing your pulling power.

≈

20 THURSDAY If money comes in, make sure it's deposited in the bank immediately, and leave your cheque book and credit cards at home in order to put temptation well out of reach. Certainly if money is owed you, you're provided with a good period for chasing it up in earnest, so get into life, Aquarius, and get cracking.

21 FRIDAY Your friends will be a little dreamy and unreliable, so if you have any sort of arrangement with them it might be a good idea to check that they haven't forgotten, because there's a strong possibility they may have done just that. Team work connected with creativity pushes ahead in leaps and bounds.

22 SATURDAY Today the Sun will be moving into the watery sign of Cancer, the area of your chart devoted to sheer hard work, relationships with workmates, and health (to a degree). If you're feeling several degrees under, don't push yourself too hard over the next couple of days. Your body will soon recover so that you can speed back into life at your normal rate. It's up to you.

23 SUNDAY If you want a day for changing your image, your mind or even your attitude, then this is it. There's an educational feel about this time, so you may be prepared to take on new studies, or perhaps adopt a new attitude to life. If your business is connected with travel, you'll be doing well throughout this day and perhaps during the evening too.

24 MONDAY Whatever occurs completely out of the blue today will be lucky for you. Be alert to all chances to enhance your life on a personal level, as well as professionally. Those of you who are going on any kind of trip today couldn't have picked a better day. Those at home will be restless and will find little excuses to keep on the go.

25 TUESDAY Although you may be surrounded by admirers, it's likely that for the most part it is your hormones which are at work rather than anything else. Do be a little careful, because you have a tendency to get carried away by the excitement of the moment and then read into situations feelings that simply do not exist. Even so, you're in for an interesting period.

26 WEDNESDAY You may change your mind more than once during this 24-hour period. Still, as an Aquarius, what's new? Those who know you well are unlikely to be fazed by your behaviour, because they're used to it by now. Romantically, a brother or a sister may make an interesting introduction. If so, it could very much be a case of lust at first sight.

27 THURSDAY It might be a good idea to examine your reasons for feeling a little disconcerted. Remember, as an Aquarian you generally prefer to travel alone. This is the way you usually find success, so why are you considering travelling with other people? Unless you have a valid reason for doing so, I suggest you sit down and have a quick re-think.

28 FRIDAY An exciting social occasion is likely to be in the offing and, while you're gadding about, a new relationship could crop up, though don't expect it to last a lifetime. If you do, you're going to be disappointed. Even so, providing you approach this day in your usual happy-go-lucky way, you'll be making a fresh start, which will prove productive.

≈

29 SATURDAY This is a time which should ideally be used for finding pleasure and fun. After all, you've been wound up for some time now and you need time for doing as you please, no matter what that might mean. So don't let yourself be bullied or cajoled into following other people's lead. Be your usual independent self, that's the only way to be.

30 SUNDAY It's likely that you'll be bursting full of energy and vitality, and are ready to take the initiative where at least one important area of life is concerned. New friends and contacts may also play an important role in your life this evening and, indirectly, lead to useful contacts or romance or, if you're really lucky, both.

JULY

Until 22 July the Sun will be drifting along in the watery sign of Cancer, the area of your chart devoted to sheer hard work. This state of affairs seems to have been going on for a rather protracted time. Not surprisingly, then, it could affect your health. If this is the case, why don't you pop around to see your doctor or dentist? If you don't want to do that, take matters into your own hands and make sure that you rest up at least two or three evenings in order to replenish and refuel. Failure to do so could lead to more serious problems.

The Sun will be moving along into Leo on 23 July, so that you will have to put other people before yourself. This won't go down a storm, I'm afraid. I'm not suggesting that you are selfish – nothing could be further from the truth – but it might be that their demands on you are simply ill-timed because you have enough on your plate and you really don't want to take on any more. Who can blame you?

≈

Mercury remains in Gemini for the first week of July, in the area of your chart devoted to creativity, sport, good times and children, too. You have plenty of chances for enjoying yourself, but remember to consider others, because if you don't you could have World War 3 breaking out, and that would be a great shame.

From 7 to 21 July Mercury will be moving along into Cancer. Once more the emphasis is on your relationships with work-mates and also on your own health. If you suspect that you're running out of steam, or feeling a little 'lacklustre', be kind to yourself and rest up so that you can take advantage of what lies ahead in future months. You don't want to mess it up now.

Mercury will be in fiery Leo from the 22nd until the end of the month. There could be new faces entering your life. If you don't take to them immediately, wait for a while before you reject them.

Venus is in your opposite sign (Leo) until 10 July, throwing a rosy glow over all of your relationships and creative work too. After this date Venus will be moving into Virgo, the area of your chart devoted to other people's finances, big business, insurance matters and shared resources. All of these matters can be pushed ahead with alacrity, so make sure that you don't let the grass grow under your feet.

Venus will be coasting through Virgo from 11 July. This is a good period in which to arrange business and financial meetings. Your ideas are likely to be well received.

Mars will be in Cancer during the first 13 days of the month. Once more, hard work is indicated here and you may be prone to danger from hot and sharp objects. Watch your food intake, too – anything that is tainted could upset your physical wellbeing and lay you low, and you wouldn't like that now, would you?

≈

After 13 July Mars will be moving into Leo. Other people may become a little cross, tense and angry over literally nothing. If this is the special person in your life, make a big fuss of them. They'll be forever grateful, and your relationship will only blossom far more than it has for some time – not a bad thing then.

The pattern made by the stars suggests that you'll be very keen to start new projects, ideas and relationships, but may lack that follow-through which is all important. If you fall into this 'bear trap', I'm afraid your progress will be stymied. You'll only have yourself to blame, so don't start lashing out at other people, that will only make you unpopular.

1 MONDAY Today you seem to be flooded with charisma and magic, so much so that others can't resist you. However, there may be a strong tendency for you to change your mind completely, to the surprise of other people, and you do take a secret delight in rocking them on their heels, don't you? Still, at least you'll have good reason for doing so, because the inspirations you receive, right now, could lead to financial gain in the future.

2 TUESDAY The stars may put a damper on your spirits; either that or the plans that you have made are prone to delay and disappointment, so the best thing you can do is to check everything. By being too casual you'll be encouraging your bad luck. Try, too, to be more patient with older members of the family, even if they are proving to be a 'real pain in the neck'. You'll only feel guilty if you tick them off.

3 WEDNESDAY There's a lively feel about this particular day. Anything which crops up completely out of the blue must be

≋

snapped up without further thought. Opportunity rarely knocks twice, you know. This evening a friend or contact will be behaving completely out of character, which intrigues you and may even lead, indirectly, to romance.

4 THURSDAY The stars will bring about changes in the lives of those closest to you. There's plenty of news flying around too, but if somebody should decide to confide in you, make sure that you respect the confidence they are placing in you and not give in to scandal-mongering. If you do, you will most certainly be found out.

5 FRIDAY The stars provide a warm happy glow over your closest intimate relationships. You've a good couple of days for forming professional partnerships if you so desire. They certainly could be successful for you. If you've been in a lengthy relationship and it's been somewhat stagnant, this is the time to chivvy it up, perhaps either by bringing it to an end, or preparing to take it a step further.

6 SATURDAY The stars today suggest you're likely to be hearing from official sources and, when you do, instead of panicking, sit down, put on your 'sensible head' and think out what needs to be done for the best. Your normal tendency to leave such things to one side can only make the situation a great deal more difficult.

7 SUNDAY Today Mercury will be moving into the water sign of Cancer and the area of your chart devoted to health (which could be a little bit tense, or up and down), and to relationships with workmates (which seem to be running a good deal more smoothly than is usually the case). Laborious work is far easier to do than usual, much to your delight.

8 MONDAY The stars provide you with a good day for getting down to hard laborious work. Admittedly this is not your favourite pastime, but life can't be all fun and games. The influence of an older person seems to be important, so any advice which is passed on to you should perhaps be listened to, even if you decide not to act on it.

9 TUESDAY For reasons best known to yourself you may be feeling a little down, depressed or even negative. This is not like you at all and it certainly won't help you to get what you want out of life, so do whatever it takes to cheer yourself up – perhaps a new hairstyle, something luscious to eat or possibly a new challenge in your spare time. Keep busy and you'll get through the day unscathed.

10 WEDNESDAY This is a good time for exploring new territories, getting away from your local surroundings and being a little more daring. In fact, the further you travel the more stimulating you will be, and the greater your chances of meeting new friends, or even finding romance. Allow the adventurer within free rein.

11 THURSDAY Today Venus will be moving into Virgo and the area of your chart devoted to insurance matters and the financial affairs of people who are closest to you, as well as artistic businesses. All these areas can be pushed in the certain knowledge that you will be doing the right thing at the right time, so get cracking.

≈

12 FRIDAY There's no point in being too ambitious or start-ing new and exciting projects, the best way to play your cards is to put the finishing touches to work, involve yourself in a bit of research and wait for a far more auspicious time for leaping into action. Impatience is likely to dog your step, but try to resist.

13 SATURDAY Many changes are going on at work, but this is no reason for you to get into a panic. Life is, after all, about change. As a rule this is your favourite word, but although you seem to be one of the most confident people under the zodiac, even you can suffer from insecurity, and that could very well be the case at this time.

14 SUNDAY Today Mars will be moving into the fiery sign of Leo, your opposite number. Oh dear! While this state of affairs exists you could be tense, bad-tempered or prone to little accidents in connection with hot or sharp objects. Do watch yourself in the kitchen and bathroom; after all, that's where most accidents occur.

15 MONDAY Gone are the doubts of yesterday, because the planets are lining up in such a way that you'll be bursting full of confidence, good-will and enthusiasm. You are positively irresistible to everybody around you. You're provided with a time for pulling yourself up yet another rung on the ladder of success – or, of course, you could spend your time sorting out problems in your personal life. The choice is entirely up to you. No doubt you'll make the wisest one at this time.

16 TUESDAY This is definitely not a time for dithering; you'll be far more inclined to start trail-blazing. No matter whom

≈

you choose to take with you into your future, you must guarantee your right to exercise more control over your fate. Aquarians are born to keep moving and progressing in life, and that often means making choices which distinguish you from everybody else.

17 WEDNESDAY You must be careful what you do and say to your friends, contacts and acquaintances, because it won't take much to upset them. In many ways you could be frustrated, because although you are bursting full of ideas, you don't seem to be provided with the opportunities to do anything constructive with them – never mind, they'll keep, though it's unlikely that this will be acceptable advice to you at this moment.

18 THURSDAY A mood of reflection could descend, and if you really understand yourself then you will have realized that it is possible to take matters to the point of absurdity. Constructive practical thought is one thing, but too much pondering can, in your case, result in insomnia and will also prove to be unproductive. When your mind is jam-packed with ideas, quite often the most lucrative of them tends to slip through, so try to stay focused.

19 FRIDAY If you're working well and in a positive frame of mind, the stars will help, but if you're not pulling your weight and have made mistakes, this is the day when they may be discovered. If the latter should be the case, it might pay you to 'come clean', because that way at least other people will respect you for your honesty. This evening you're at your most sensitive, so choose your company carefully.

≈

20 SATURDAY There's a certain amount of muddle and you're definitely prone to absentmindedness. It looks as if there's too much going on in your head. Your brain could be likened to a demented carousel which is completely out of control. Do whatever it takes to calm yourself down and think things through to a practical conclusion before you move on to another subject or job. In this way, you'll side-step difficulties.

21 SUNDAY Minor changes are clearly taking place and, although you may gain, you could also lose. It might be a good idea for you to avoid the more expensive shops, because you could develop a case of love at first sight for something completely impractical and then, at a later date, wonder why your bank account is mysteriously empty. You never have learned how to keep accounts, have you, Aquarius? Well, it's all part of being a member of your sign, I suppose.

22 MONDAY Today Mercury will be moving into your opposite sign, Leo, livening up the minds of those closest to you. They'll be running around like cats who have lost their tail, and may come to you in an effort to sort them out. Of course, you'll be happy to do so without expecting any kind of gratitude, because that's the sort of person you are.

23 TUESDAY The stars suggest that you're thinking seriously about becoming deeply committed to one of your relationships. You need this day for thought, because if you rush off half-cocked, as you sometimes do, it tends to lead to an accident-prone emotional life, as I'm sure you know by now. There also seems to be the influence of an older person, which is all to the good. Maybe a more experienced head can help you sort out your jumbled thoughts or feelings.

≈

24 WEDNESDAY Today is the day of the full Moon, in the airy sign of Aquarius. It won't pay to begin anything fresh. Instead, do the opposite: sort out the finishing touches to all those little jobs, relationships and everything else that you have left undone. If you've an Aquarian in your life, they may be making some extra demands. It's up to you to know when enough is enough.

25 THURSDAY Today is a good time for those of you who work in the service industries, or those who have fallen behind in your workload, because you're going to have plenty of energy and the willpower to catch up and surpass yourself. It's a good day for making arrangements to have your teeth or your body checked out by the dentist or doctor because, after all, you are human. Though you tend to think you can go on and on and on without sufficient rest, this isn't strictly true and, if you're honest, you'll admit it. When you fall by the wayside and become prone to infection or illness, it's nearly always a case of being run down.

26 FRIDAY With any luck you should be surrounded by a certain amount of co-operation, peace and harmony. Friends, contacts and acquaintances will be doing everything in their power to help you out in any way they can, so if you want advice or assistance in any way, shape or form, don't be slow to come forward. Luckily, you're not usually hampered by foolish pride, so don't make this day an exception. It's your contacts which will be invaluable at the moment.

27 SATURDAY It's a time to focus your mind on your ambitions. Mentally you've been exploring options that can now come to fruition. Any struggles in your life can be solved by

≈

simply sorting out your priorities. It's time to recognize whether people are playing with your ideas, or are willing to make a commitment. There really is no room for reluctance on the chosen path, not this time anyway.

28 SUNDAY This is a time when you may be taking on new interests, studies or hobbies which are likely to be of an intellectual nature. Affairs connected with younger people can be tackled satisfactorily; you will know what needs to be done, and at what time. This evening unexpected visitors may pop in.

29 MONDAY The stars suggest changes in the area of your life connected with children, pleasure and romance. Those attracted to you take you seriously at their peril, as you're simply testing your 'pulling power'. The only trouble is that you're not letting them in on this. If you have arrangements with anybody this evening, don't let them down without making that all-important phone call, or you'll be at the bottom of their popularity poll for some time to come, and that would never do.

30 TUESDAY Today you're about to throw off recent introspection and throw yourself wholeheartedly into the swim of things. You'll be taking on the role of leader at this time. Because of this, romantic and social activity is likely to be instigated by your good self. Your opposite number will also notice the extra depth to your personality and will be responding in a positive way.

31 WEDNESDAY Those closest to you, both at work and at home and in your friendship circle, are certainly lively and full of good ideas, so why don't you give them a listen? You might be quite glad that you did. If you have a Gemini or a Virgo in your life, these could be the ideal people to go to for advice.

AUGUST

Until 22 August the Sun will be drifting along in the fiery sign of Leo, the area of your chart devoted to partnerships. This section of your chart certainly seems to be overcrowded. However, the Sun sees that other people are in a good mood, so if you need to approach them for any reason at all, don't hesitate to do so.

On the 23rd the Sun will be moving on into Virgo, the area of your chart devoted to people you are financially dependent upon, insurance matters and big business such as the Stock Exchange. If you want to make any moves in any of these sides of life, then get cracking immediately. Don't let the grass grow under your feet.

Mercury is in Leo for the first five days of the month; once more, other people's affairs are quite lively, and this seems to affect you, but not for much longer. Quite frankly, you can't wait for matters to return to normal so that you can start looking after your own business.

After 6 August Mercury will be moving into Virgo. This is a good time for pushing for contracts if they happen to be in the pipeline. Furthermore, if you're working as part of a team, there might be a minor breakthrough – but nothing world-shattering, so don't get your hopes up too high.

Venus will be in Virgo for the first six days of August; this is a good time for presenting your new ideas to others. Don't be intimidated and, if you don't immediately get the reaction

≈

you were hoping for, don't be disappointed – you know you are in the right.

From 7 August Venus will be sailing through airy Libra, suggesting creative work as well as socializing. If you have a partner, you'd better keep yourself under control or you may find yourself in the doghouse.

Mars will be roaring through the fiery sign of Leo all August. You might find yourself at loggerheads with others if you insist on trying to impose your views. Keep your crazier ideas to yourself for the moment, because they will only be rejected. Just hang fire and wait for a better moment.

The pattern made by the stars seems to be focusing on other people. This is perhaps not the best time, then, to push ahead with anything in your own life which is too sensitive to change, because to do so could mean that things fall through. After all, Aquarius, life is about timing. You must make sure that you take this into consideration whenever you do anything of major importance.

1 THURSDAY You'll be putting your heart and soul into work, and it's a good time for sorting out the complicated financial side of your life and facing up to some basic home truths – mainly that you don't have an unlimited supply of money, not unless you're making it yourself. As always, in all areas of life, this is one of those times when the Moon's position suggests you can make a fresh start, so don't hesitate.

2 FRIDAY It looks as if the temperature is rising in one of your relationships. You might have to reconsider how to handle a particular person who remains stubbornly determined to stand their ground. This is the moment to take action and persuade other people that you mean business. It's your turn to express how you feel and grab your chance to chase your aims without undue interference from others.

3 SATURDAY It looks as if passion is stirring one of your closest relationships. This could prove to be something of a double-edged sword. Shaking people out of their laziness seems to be one means of proving your point, although once you have declared your feelings, you'll have to deal with the consequences. What seems to be at stake isn't paying the final bill when it comes to leaving, but whether those you care about are prepared to enter into the spirit of things.

4 SUNDAY Today the stars pile pressure on your already over-loaded workload. There might not be enough space for a well-earned rest, but a change of scene could give you a fresh perspective on a current problem. The stars suggest that your path to happiness lies in being true to yourself. Very soon you'll discover that nothing can stand in your way.

5 MONDAY You'd be well advised not to take the promises or commitments of other people too seriously, because their judgement is totally off and their enthusiasm is running riot. No doubt their company will be enjoyable and, as long as they stay in a flighty frame of mind, you can turn this aspect around and thoroughly enjoy yourself – it's up to you.

6 TUESDAY Today Mercury will be moving into the earthy sign of Virgo, the area of your chart devoted to the financial affairs of other people, the Stock Exchange and maybe team effort, to a degree. Changes in these areas are OK by the stars, but don't go to extremes or somebody will bring you up short.

≈

7 WEDNESDAY There may be a certain anxiety in you as to whether someone close to you is really pulling their weight, or whether it is you who is carrying around the lion's share of the problems and decision-making, when ideally they should be divided between the two of you. If you're dissatisfied with this situation, now is the time to speak up, or forever hold your peace.

8 THURSDAY The stars are providing you with a time for intense concentration, decision-making and also taking a dispassionate look at the way you are feeling about a particular relationship. When you do, you may realize the direction in which you are going is not one you want to follow, in which case it's time to do something about it.

9 FRIDAY The Moon will be putting you in an overly idealistic frame of mind, and your expectations of others go beyond the bounds of reason. If you can recognize this in yourself, lower your sights; otherwise you are sure to be disappointed at a later date, and this doesn't sit well on your shoulders, does it Aquarius?

10 SATURDAY Today you will see somebody in their true colours. Once you are aware of their intentions and desires, you can either bury the hatchet or start on a different course. There's also a sparky feel to new relationships, which encourage spontaneous decisions. In fact, however impulsive you might seem, other people may not realize that events have been leading up to this course of action for quite some time now.

11 SUNDAY There's likely to be a dramatic change of outlook or mind today, because your butterfly head is constantly on a quest for the new or the 'different'. Others may not realize that you mean business at this time, so you'll have to find some way of letting them know that you're not about to allow yourself to be messed around in any way, shape or form.

12 MONDAY Other people will be full of admiration for your originality, and this will result in a nice warm glow inside. Aquarians who are waiting to hear from somebody abroad are unlikely to be disappointed. This is certainly a day when literally anything can happen and probably will, so it's just as well that you're born under this adaptable air sign.

13 TUESDAY If you're a freelance worker, make that crucial call because it could make all the difference. If not, greet new faces on your social scene with a certain amount of warmth, as well as curiosity. Remember, there's a tendency for you to regard strangers as specimens, rather than living, breathing human beings.

14 WEDNESDAY You may experience a couple of days when you feel the need to retire from the hustle and bustle of life and sort out your own thoughts. Naturally, if you're working this just may not be possible, in which case may I suggest that you plan a quiet evening, during which you can please yourself in whatever way you choose.

15 THURSDAY It's quite likely that you may run out of either energy or enthusiasm today at work. This may create an unfortunate impression. A certain insecurity may dog your every step, but if this is case remind yourself it's only the planets playing up and this will soon pass away. In the mean time, make your plans but don't leap into action.

≋

16 FRIDAY There may be a slowing down of your plans, but this can only work in your favour in the end. You'll find those who are closest to you in a very serious mood, and they want to pin you down to a decision, or simply pick your brains to find out what your intentions are. There's no way you can 'duck and dive' this, Aquarius, it's time to own up and be truthful.

17 SATURDAY You seem to be slap bang in the middle of all the action and limelight. Make sure you're looking good, because you'll most certainly be feeling great. Use this day for pushing those ambitions further forward towards to your ultimate goal and you won't waste time. This evening you'll probably feel like spoiling yourself – the stars give you permission to do so, just as long as you don't go stark raving mad. Steer the middle road where money is concerned and you'll remain solvent.

18 SUNDAY If ever there was a time for deciding exactly what and whom you want out of your life, this is it, so don't waste it. Your concentration is increased, so even the most laborious of jobs can be tackled with a willing heart, for a change. If you're trying to gain support from a superior or a more experienced person, you won't be disappointed because they'll be impressed with what you have to say.

19 MONDAY The more ambitious side of your personality will be apparent to all those around. If you believe in your ideas and suggestions, you won't be put off by more negative souls in your social circle at work. Push ahead with anything that is important to you, because this is one time when you can do yourself a great deal of good. If you're out of work, this is an ideal day for doing something constructive about it.

≈

20 TUESDAY You may be worrying unnecessarily about an emotional matter. You're blowing minor disagreements into full-scale wars, and can't see the proverbial wood for the trees. It might be a good idea to keep your grey matter occupied so that you have neither the time nor inclination to fall into the trap the stars are setting for you. Whatever you decide to do is, of course, entirely up to you.

21 WEDNESDAY Romantically, you couldn't ask for more encouraging signals than those coming from the stars at the moment. However, you can't afford to ignore matters related to your own personal security. Being able to grasp the nitty-gritty and smoothing out differences of opinion is vital if you are to rise to your chosen heights. To improve a relationship you might need to open up your mind as well as your heart.

22 THURSDAY Today is the day of the full Moon and it occurs in your own sign, so if you wake up feeling grumpy, bad-tempered, stressed or generally out of sorts, you now know what to blame. This is certainly not a time for innovative ventures or taking any kind of risk. Instead, make it your business to put the finishing touches to all those little jobs and projects you've left undone. That's the way to go.

23 FRIDAY This is a day when the Sun will be moving into earthy Virgo, the area of your chart devoted to big business, the Stock Exchange and relationships with your workmates. Somebody who has been disagreeable, perhaps envious of your success, begins to see sense and you form a close relationship, which can be no bad thing.

≈

24 SATURDAY You probably meet up with some kind of difficulty in getting your point across right now. Whatever flares up between yourself and a partner, or a close workmate, is not a sign of enduring disagreements, but a flashpoint which strengthens the potential of this relationship. By the time the day is through, your mind will be clear of doubt and your mental powers will be heightened.

25 SUNDAY This is a day that could produce all sorts of unexpected episodes which leave you gasping for an answer. Workmates or associates seem to be making a stand, and you're left wondering why they are causing such a rumpus. There's little you can do to remedy the situation, so console yourself with those who care about you.

26 MONDAY It's possible that you now realize that someone close is discontented or worried that you have preferred to ignore them. You realize that pushing ahead with your own life is not the thing to do and you are ready to admit your mistakes. If you're totally unattached it's an ideal time for being more sociable; other people will be naturally drawn to your quick wit, your enthusiasm and your nice nature. You may even be picking up some useful professional tips while out having fun.

27 TUESDAY Do a little double-checking where artistic projects and your social life are concerned, because a muddle could crop up completely out of the blue. Now that you are prepared, there is no excuse for falling into this trap. Mind you, you are one of the most adaptable people under the zodiac, so it takes a great deal to throw you off your stride.

≈

28 WEDNESDAY There's a cozy aspect between the planets and a strong emphasis on gathering information. Certainly, if you're a student you will have flashes of inspiration which will impress not only your tutors but also your college mates. On the other hand, if your work is creative you'll have other people's undying admiration. It's very much a case of whether you dare to reveal matters that are mulling around in your head. The advice from the stars is to push ahead and do so.

29 THURSDAY You may not be able to stick to routine – whatever that is! Change could create a certain amount of transformation, or even upheaval, but as an Aquarian you delight in anything which breaks the dull, boring routine, and are able to adjust in record time. This evening will be an ideal time for visiting friends who live close by, even if it's only to catch up on local gossip.

30 FRIDAY You may find other people unreliable and changeable – now you know how it feels when the rest of us have to do deal with you! Luckily, though, you invariably welcome anything – with the possible exception of boring routine – so this won't faze you for very long. This evening, if you're out socializing, it's new faces you'll be drawn to, rather than the old crowd. Possibly you've heard all their life stories already and you want something new to explore. This person won't be difficult to find.

31 SATURDAY There seems to be a minor new cycle happening in one of your intensely personal relationships. In some cases this may work out negatively and you may find yourself confronted with an ultimatum – which, of course, you will resent and rebel against like crazy. On the other hand, if

≈

you are totally fancy-free a new face could set those hormones coursing through your veins. If so, I can't think of a nicer way to end any month. This seems to be a great time for making fresh starts, for discarding old habits and taking on fresh outlooks and advice – which, Aquarius, just for once you'll be pleased to do.

SEPTEMBER

Until 22 September the Sun will be coasting along in the earthy sign of Virgo, the area of your chart devoted to matters related to big business, the Stock Exchange and people you are financially dependent upon. However, just as long as you remain polite when dealing with such people, you'll have nothing to fear.

On the 23rd the Sun will be drifting along in the airy sign of Libra, the area of your chart devoted to friends, team effort and perhaps insurance matters. Just for once, you won't isolate yourself from other people; you want to be as sociable as you possibly can be, and because of this will be making new friends, as well as pleasing your old ones.

Mercury will be coasting through Libra all month. There is an emphasis on education and matters relating to far-off places. If you have been looking for the answer to a problem or dilemma, it is possible a friend from abroad may be able to help you out. Unfortunately, after 14 September Mercury goes into retrograde movement, disrupting channels of communication – take particular care of what you say and write. Travellers could also face difficulties, so keep on your mettle while this state of affairs persists.

Venus will remain in Libra for the first seven days of the month, so that matters related to abroad may be quite important. Be alert for foreign-sounding accidents, they could benefit you in some way.

From 8 September onwards, Venus will have moved into the water sign of Scorpio, the area of your chart devoted to home, property and family affairs. It's also a good time for those whose work is connected with home comforts, perhaps home improvements. If this applies to you, you're in for a good time.

Mars will be in Virgo all month, so there could be a certain amount of tension and argument with officials, bureaucrats, the tax man and perhaps even your bank manager. It will pay you to keep a civil tongue in your head, so see that you do, Aquarius. It's no good 'trying to steal a march' on them, this just won't happen. They've got more information at their fingertips than you have, so it wouldn't be a good idea to 'try it on'.

The pattern made by the stars is a very scattered one, which suggests that you'll be trying to be all things to all people. Not only that, but you will place an unbelievably heavy burden on your shoulders where work matters are concerned. Sit down and work out what is important, make a list if necessary, putting your top priority at the top and grading the others downwards till you can finally see in black and white what needs to be done next. Once you've done this, you're likely to be a good deal more successful – if only we can persuade you to do so, which, let's face it, is a bit doubtful.

1 SUNDAY As a flirtatious Aquarian, you sometimes send out confused signals which could land you in hot water. Luckily, right now you'll be more than happy to expose your inner desires in love and bring about chances to enrich your life through your relationships. For some of you it's time to be

≈

honest with yourself and be ready for relationships to grow in importance. Either way, it looks as if there's a happy glow over this side of life, which makes you feel a good deal happier.

2 MONDAY There's a strong possibility that the planets will make you feel determined to prove yourself to all and sundry. This seems to be a very productive day in your working life. There's a sense of realism which is guiding you, and you'll be rewarded for your efforts rather than simply for being in the right place at the right time.

3 TUESDAY It looks as if the stars are about to expand your workload, and you'll be feeling far more enthusiastic about what you do. If your present work is lacking opportunities to prove yourself, you will find the courage to aim for something more challenging. Relationships at work will be encouraging and supportive. It's a good time to learn from other people – you may find a great teacher.

4 WEDNESDAY You can expect a very lively feel about this day, and this will encourage positive attitudes as well as high spirits. When it comes to daily routine, expect to be interrupted on several occasions, though as a changeable air sign you will probably welcome anything which takes your nose away from the grindstone.

5 THURSDAY There's a sensible, down-to-earth feel about the day. This is certainly a time for assessing your progress and deciding whether or not you want to make a change. If you do, lay down some plans now. This evening, the influence of an older and more experienced person seems to surround you, and you're receiving some good advice, but are you going to listen?

≈

6 FRIDAY Even if you're not at work, ambitions and plans to get ahead are very much in the centre of your thoughts. Others may find you dreamy or even absent-minded, so why don't you discuss your deepest wishes and hopes with them? They are sure to offer lots of encouragement.

7 SATURDAY Today is the day of the new Moon, and it falls in the gritty sign of Virgo, the area of your chart devoted to insurance matters, people you are financially dependent upon and team effort. There may be some kind of breakthrough in at least one area, and this should at least make this a fine day. As always, of course, with new Moons you can make fresh starts.

8 SUNDAY Today Venus will be moving into the water sign of Scorpio, the area of your chart devoted to ambition. There's a rosy glow over relationships with people you meet during your professional life. Some of you may even fall in love with a new colleague, but if you've got a mate at home for heaven's sake be careful, otherwise you'll land yourself in hot water right up to your neck.

9 MONDAY The stars seem to be roaring ahead today with extra drive and determination. This is a time when you won't let anyone, or anything, stand in your way. Recently you may have been withdrawn or perhaps had confidence knocked out of you, but right now your creative self-expression helps you to bounce back in no uncertain fashion. You definitely have a feeling that anything is possible – and you're right.

10 TUESDAY Today it's definitely a case of whom you know and not what you know that counts. If you're a freelance worker, get in touch with all of your contacts. You could unearth an opportunity. The same advice applies if you're out of work. This evening you could do worse than visit a club with an old friend, because this is where you're most likely to find romance.

11 WEDNESDAY You may be experiencing a rather dreamy time in connection with romance. Just make sure you don't get completely carried away – you can be extremist on occasion, you know. If you're completely unattached it might be a good idea to keep a high profile, particularly on the work front, because it's through a colleague that you could meet a special person. Mind you, other people may be deceptive; to protect yourself, see what you can do to check out their marital status.

12 THURSDAY You could be given to extravagance; if so, you are sure to live to regret it. Make sure that you balance your books and check if you have sufficient money to cover expenses before even thinking about spending on frivolous items. If you've a thorny financial problem that's worrying you, go to somebody experienced; they will be able to lend a helping hand with some good words of advice.

13 FRIDAY A great time for getting support and encouragement from other people. This evening, visit those who make you laugh. You need to let off steam, and it beats chewing your fingernails down to the elbow.

14 SATURDAY Oh dear! Today Mercury decides to go into retrograde movement; from here on in you really must think twice before signing on the dotted line or undertaking any kind of unnecessary travel. Furthermore, if you've a Virgo or a Gemini in your life, they could downright awkward from here on in. If you show extreme patience and also let them know that you care about them, then you will be minimizing any difficulties.

15 SUNDAY You tend to become a little withdrawn today; still, we all need a period of reflection from time to time, so that we can cope with day-to-day problems. Do yourself a favour and plan a lazy evening regardless of what other people say.

16 MONDAY You start off the day in a reflective and maybe even grumpy mood, but as the hours pass you gradually become your usual chatty and gregarious self. Get out into the world and give the rest of us the benefit of your company.

17 TUESDAY You're much softer in your approach to other people, and the day promises to bring some passion back into your life through a romance with somebody who is looking for a deep, intense relationship. If you're already involved, you still may not be able to understand the person closest to you, who is being secretive for reasons best known to themselves. No doubt, all will be revealed in the fullness of time. If, on the other hand, you decide that your current partnership is lacking in lustre, you might find yourself attracted elsewhere.

18 WEDNESDAY You can expect friends, contacts and partners to be a little disorganized, so if you have arrangements with them don't leave anything to chance. Get on the phone and check, this way you'll avoid standing for hours waiting for someone who simply doesn't bother to turn up. It's a hectic day at work, so you may decide to get an early night.

≈

19 THURSDAY You're flooded with solar power, confidence and energy. This is a time for occupying centre-stage and making a few cheeky demands, because others have been putting upon you, for some time, so this is a day for turning a situation around and going after your own interests. See what you can do.

20 FRIDAY Luckily you're not the type who is starry-eyed about relationships, but your ability to spot people's weaknesses, as well as their strengths, gives you a realistic appreciation of those you love. So, if you've been putting up with somebody else's philandering, you will not be slow to come forward and remind them of their responsibilities to you. If they don't listen, they'll be jettisoned from your life.

21 SATURDAY This is the day of the full Moon, and it occurs in the water sign of Pisces, the area of your chart devoted to money. There seems to be a drain on your resources. Luckily, you're unlikely to spend unnecessarily while in the working environment, but this evening a new friend may have some expensive ideas. Regardless of how much you want to stay friendly with them, it wouldn't be a good idea to sling yourself into bankruptcy – I think you'll agree. Mind you, full Moons can be used for putting the finishing touches to literally anything.

22 SUNDAY You certainly seem to be drawing a good deal of attention from other people right now, and you are also more decisive, which is no bad thing. However, it's never good to believe you're always right, as you sometimes do. Nevertheless, you are ready to listen to other people's problems and ideas, and also, perhaps, to co-operate with them.

≈

By working with them you'll be making leaps and bounds in your own ambitions, whether they be professional or personal.

23 MONDAY Today the Sun will be moving into the airy sign of Libra, the area of your chart devoted to long-distance travel, foreign affairs and legal matters. Any, or all, of these can be pushed with alacrity over the next few days or so, in the certain knowledge you're doing the right thing.

24 TUESDAY It looks as if activity on the home front is at a frantic pace; possibly you are the one who is acting the role of host/hostess for a social occasion and are making necessary preparations. Make sure that everybody else mucks in with you, because there's no reason why you should struggle on alone, I think you'll agree.

25 WEDNESDAY Today's stars suggest there may be a special occasion you're really looking forward to. If so, it will live up to your high expectations and may even provide you with a chance of finding romance. Of course, if you already have a partner you'll need to control your 'wandering eye' because, as an Aquarian, there's nothing you like better than to live dangerously occasionally. This often proves to be your downfall.

26 THURSDAY You seem to be devoting yourself to pleasure, romance and fun, which is just as well because this is a time when you will have many opportunities in these areas. Those of you who are putting finishing touches to any kind of work will do so in record time, and are likely to be joining colleagues around lunch time and swapping gossip. However, if you're hoping to drive at any point, you need to be very

≈

careful. Far better to spend money on hiring a cab, rather than risk being caught drink-driving.

27 FRIDAY Today it looks as if there will be a chance for you to pick up a bargain, so perhaps you're being a lot wiser than most people believe. Many of you may have a hectic evening because you're trying to cram so much activity into it, but don't go overboard otherwise you'll become inefficient and other people will criticize you, even though they've no right to.

28 SATURDAY Life will be far less complicated than it has been for quite a while. You'll probably experience that feeling of taking one step forward and half a dozen backwards, but this phase is now at an end and you can push ahead with all your hopes, wishes and dreams in no matter area they may lie.

29 SUNDAY The lives of those closest to you are prone to interruption and delay, so take a few safety precautions. Ring around and make sure everybody knows where they're supposed to be and at what time. If you are single, you may be introduced to an interesting individual who will certainly start your heart pumping – what a lovely thing to happen.

30 MONDAY This is a time when you must not allow other people to make you feel lazy if you have decided to relax and do a bit of thinking, instead of acting all the time. No doubt, after an hour or so of inactivity you'll soon be itching to get started again anyway, and although you have promised yourself an early night, it's doubtful that you'll stick to this, because you're in the mood for fun and games – and why not?

≈

OCTOBER

Until 23 October the Sun will be drifting through the air sign of Libra, the area of your chart devoted to matters related to abroad, higher education, insurance matters and people you may be financially dependent upon. For the most part this planet is well starred, but use the Daily Guides if you've got anything particularly important to do in connection with these matters.

From 24 October the Sun will be drifting along in the water sign of Scorpio, the zenith point of your chart. It looks as if you're in for a couple of weeks of real hard slog. Make it easy on yourself and accept this rather than baulking against it, because that will only make matters worse. On the upside, workmates are willing to help you out and will also be extending social invitations, so you've got quite a lot to look forward to one way or the other.

Mercury moves into Libra on 11 October, so once more we have an emphasis on foreign affairs and higher education. You can push very easily with these matters and not run up against any sort of hang-ups or difficulties whatsoever, so that's good news.

Venus is located in Scorpio, the zenith point of your chart. It looks as if there's a great deal of co-operation going on at work, and perhaps you'll be mixing business with pleasure too, which will be fun. However, be warned, Venus goes in retrograde movement on the 10th, so after this date artistic affairs, romance and creative work will all become complicated. Try to keep calm when this happens, because that's the only way you'll be able to sort matters out.

Mars will be in Virgo until 15 October, therefore there's a certain amount of tension where team effort is concerned.

≈

Insurance matters and people you are financially dependent upon may not be as co-operative as they have been recently, therefore it's not a good idea to take anything for granted. If you do, I think you're going to be seriously disappointed, Aquarius. Furthermore, because of the position of Mars, it may be your male friends who are stirring up a 'hornet's nest'. Don't take them too seriously. Try to stay relaxed and you can overcome this.

The pattern made by the stars is a rather scattered one, which seems to suggest that you'll be much better at starting things than finishing them, a pitfall many of us suffer from. However, if you can be scrupulous and double-check everything, you'll be able to sleep at nights and will also please your boss and colleagues, too. This isn't the kindest month you've ever experienced, nevertheless neither is it disastrous; we must be grateful for small mercies.

1 TUESDAY It's a changeable day on the work front; you need to be as flexible as you possibly can. Don't shirk hard work but, on the other hand, don't be the one to volunteer. If you are tempted to talk your way out of a difficult situation, remember that even white lies go against you. You may decide to cancel an arrangement this evening because you have simply run out of steam. If so, it's a very wise move.

2 WEDNESDAY The stars put you in an odd mood. You're irritated by money difficulties and, just for once, you don't feel you can trust a close friend. This could be a touch of paranoia setting in here; the best thing you can do is to keep your head constantly preoccupied, both during the day and in the evening. If a chance to socialize with a neighbour crops up,

≈

grasp it with both hands: it will be good for keeping yourself busy and, besides, you'll meet new, interesting people.

3 THURSDAY This is a time when you're likely to be rushed off your feet. Luckily you have lots of stamina, which is just as well, because you are most certainly going to need it. There will be a tendency for you to become physically attracted to people you meet through your job.

4 FRIDAY It looks as if other people will be in control of situations, both at work and at home, over the next day or so. Still, at least you'll be provided with the chance to meet new faces and, if you're already close to somebody, your intimacy will be growing and this will give you a great deal of satisfaction.

5 SATURDAY Thankfully, today Mercury resumes direct movement. This is good news, because you can now turn your attention to paperwork, documents, travel and perhaps new members in your circle without feeling you're doing the wrong thing. If you've a Virgo or a Gemini in your life, they're bound to be high spirits.

6 SUNDAY Today is the day of the new Moon, and it falls in the airy sign of Libra, the area of your chart devoted to fun, sport, children and casual romance. There's quite a lot to look forward to here. It's time to make fresh beginnings without fear that you'll be doing the wrong thing, because you most certainly won't.

7 MONDAY You're certainly going to be popular today, and you should try to look on the bright side of life. Put some extra effort into your appearance, particularly if you're

≈

fancy-free: always remember that first impressions count in a big way; this is especially true at this time. If you're in a relationship, your partner will be in a sensitive frame of mind, so open up your big warm heart and let them step in.

8 TUESDAY Your head is bursting full of good ideas for the future, but money complications and obstacles may just stop you in your tracks. If you can be prepared to make slower progress, you'll be doing yourself a big favour. In the mean time, lay down your master plan and make sure you have attended to all the practicalities; then things will tick along nicely. This evening you may opt for catching up with jobs around the home, or perhaps sitting down and watching your favourite programme on television.

9 WEDNESDAY Today could bring stress and minor disagreements. Perhaps you'll fall out with somebody over cash or an emotional issue. However, this is no bad thing, because opinions always need to be aired, otherwise they have a way of growing out of proportion and assuming 'crises' dimensions. If you're fancy-free this evening, there's a strong chance of romance. Treat this in the right way, in a lighthearted and good-natured frame of mind.

10 THURSDAY Unfortunately, today Venus goes into retrograde movement, so from here on in matters related to abroad and higher education, as well as perhaps the Stock Exchange, could get unbelievably complicated. The best thing to do is to stick to routine, that way things should run smoothly enough. However, even this evening the planets could be out to get you. If you meet anyone special, you'd better check their credentials. They may not be telling the truth.

≈

11 FRIDAY Today Saturn will be going into retrograde movement, in a rather secretive area of your chart. You may be getting lots of good ideas which you believe are due to your intuition, but in actual fact you don't have all the facts at your fingertips and you could make a fool of yourself, so take care. Older people in your circle will try to avoid you, not because they don't want to see you, but because their life is full to bursting and they can't cope with any more dramas, so be understanding if you possibly can.

12 SATURDAY Mercury is now in Libra, so once more we have the emphasis on foreign affairs, higher education and those workmates of yours. Mind you, everything seems to be starred in a very satisfactory and positive way, so there's very little for you to fear.

13 SUNDAY The stars today could bring a spot of luck. What's more, you're thinking outside of yourself for a change. and considering the possibility of moving on in at least one area of life. This is an ideal time for doing so, because your inspirations and intuitions are spot on and no one can tell you how to run your life. You're managing very well on your own, thank you very much.

14 MONDAY If you're dealing with foreigners, or planning any kind of trip, this should be a successful day. All Aquarians will have reason to feel much happier about future prospects, because something will happen today that could set the adrenalin pounding through their veins. Be on the alert for opportunities.

≈

15 TUESDAY Develop a need for self-improvement. For some of you this may simply be a case of a new outfit or a hairstyle, but for others there may be a deep desire to improve the mind. If so, don't hesitate to sign up on a fresh course of learning. A good time, too, for those involved in education as well as travel.

16 WEDNESDAY Today Mars will be moving into the airy sign of Libra, the area of your chart devoted foreign travel and legal matters, which could become tense and rather difficult to handle. Furthermore, if you do have a Libran in your life, be wary because sparks are likely to fly over literally nothing. Somebody's got to keep a sense of proportion, and it might as well be you.

17 THURSDAY It's unlikely that you'll be getting on with a partner. The best thing to do is not to expect them to agree automatically to what you want, either at home or at work; in this way you'll be more considerate and possibly be able to avoid serious breaks in the relationship. Those of you who are planning to move soon should consider thoroughly and well, but not take any action during this particular day. If you're feeling unsettled, don't worry; it's only the stars stirring you up.

18 FRIDAY It might be a good idea to watch your possessions when you are on the move from place to place. Avoid any so-called 'bargains' when out and about in shopping centres. Head straight for the necessities and double-check your change. In this way you'll be protected from any real loss. Quite obviously, then, this is certainly not the time for putting cash at risk, particularly on foolish gambling.

19 SATURDAY Hopefully you'll be delighted to hear that the planets seem to be in a good mood for once. This means that even though finances have been complicated recently, they seem to be righting themselves. Mind you, of course, a lot of this has to do with your own efforts. Things don't happen by themselves, so give yourself a pat on the back. Lastly, it's not a great time for signing important documents, for they won't enrich you as much as you expect.

20 SUNDAY You'll need your splendid common sense today, because you're likely to be faced with a string of ups and downs. You are sure to experience a stream of bright ideas which may tempt you into being more adventurous and lead to some interesting developments. You're on an emotional high, too, but perhaps just too explosive, so you'd better put your partners on red alert.

21 MONDAY Today is the day of the full Moon, and it occurs in the fiery sign of Aries, suggesting that you keep a firm grasp on your belongings. You may be rather careless with your property and lose things, or you may be too generous with your hard-earned cash. If there is a Gemini in your life, give them a wide berth today.

22 TUESDAY Partners and your family seem to be pulling you in opposite directions, leaving you unable to move either way. Take time out to visit friends you trust, leaving this thorny situation to sort itself out. The good news is that the planets are making you more emotional, romantic and flexible, especially where other people are concerned, and that can't be bad.

≈

23 WEDNESDAY The planets will certainly be livening up your ability to express yourself, keep you on the move physically and bring new contacts and friends into your life. You'll find little reasons to keep on the go, because brief encounters are a possibility. You certainly won't waste your time. A good day for the Aquarian who works in sales and who wants to go to any sort of meeting.

24 THURSDAY Today the Sun will be moving into Scorpio, the area of your chart devoted to career or profession. Certainly you're going to have much more confidence than you usually do, and you won't hesitate to offer your bright ideas to superiors who will make a note of them for the future. You'll be building up some brownie points here, and who can blame you?

25 FRIDAY With your usual careful planning you're certainly going to be reaping the rewards of your efforts sooner than you think. A possible pitfall is that you're going to throw yourself body and soul into work, and if you're going to do this, how on earth are you going to have any time left for those special people in your life? The answer to this is that you probably won't, but it might be a good idea, my Aquarian friend, to make sure that you are there when you are needed.

26 SATURDAY There's one pitfall today which you must be aware of. There may be some problems or bad feelings where your family is concerned. Looking on the brighter side, though, you could make this day and evening work for you by sitting down with loved ones, sorting out differences or laying down plans for the future. Whatever you do, don't skulk off to a corner and refuse to communicate with anybody for reasons best known to yourself. That's the worst thing to do.

27 SUNDAY The stars are speeding up everybody around you so that you come to believe that possibly you're working in slow motion. There's a credit side to this, because those closest to you will certainly be in a physical mood, so if you're in one of your 'lusty' moods you won't have any difficulty finding satisfaction. I doubt that you'll be going very far this evening.

28 MONDAY There's a possibility that friction may be sparked off between yourself and a colleague, friend or close partner; don't allow this to rub you up the wrong way. Remember there are times, and this is one of them, when we take people's words too much to heart. In the mean time they have forgotten what they've said and gone on their way, while we are left brooding and hurt. The main thing to remember is to get your priorities in the right order and see what you can do to carve out a niche for yourself.

29 TUESDAY Too often you're the sort of person who is left to point out all of the facts to other people, but doing so today won't win friends or influence others. Luckily you're going to be so caught up in the fun side of life over the next couple of days that your feet will have trouble staying on the ground. Whatever is influencing you to change direction, you must make sure you see eye to eye with those closest to you.

30 WEDNESDAY You seem to be on the point of no return regarding a plan or idea that relies on somebody else to get it off the ground. Firm but gentle words might be the order of

≈

the day. You mustn't let anyone ruffle your feathers too much. What is, in fact, beginning to get off the ground will bring you a new approach to life which relies far less on pleasing others and will bring you a greater sense of personal fulfilment.

31 THURSDAY Satisfaction can be elusive for you, especially where relationships are concerned. There are times when you begin to wish for what is unattainable. Today you may be forced to question whether or not the grass really is greener on the other side of the fence. What happens today should convince even you that, by committing yourself to somebody else, or a new sense of direction, and believing in it, you stand a greater chance of success than continually harking back to the past will do.

NOVEMBER

Until 21 November the Sun will be drifting along in the water sign of Scorpio, the area of your chart dedicated to your profession or work. You seem to be a little 'one-pointed'. If you're going to concentrate all your energies in this way, no doubt it will help your career but it won't please your loved ones. They will be making loud noises about neglect, so do think twice.

From 22 November the Sun will be drifting along through the fiery sign of Sagittarius, the area of your chart devoted to buying, selling, affairs related to brothers and sisters and short journeys, all of which should be thoroughly enjoyable. If you've fallen out with a sibling recently, now is the time for kissing and making up – always assuming, of course, that you want to.

Mercury will be sailing along in the water sign of Scorpio up until 18 November, so there are likely to be lots of changes

≈

in connection with your job. Nothing drastic, so you don't have to worry about that, just enough to keep you lively.

On 19 November Mercury will be moving into Sagittarius, the area of your chart devoted to team effort, friendship, acquaintances and friends. This is definitely going to be a time when it's whom you know, not what you know, that's really going to count. Bear this in mind, especially when you're attending meetings.

Venus stubbornly stays in Scorpio all month, at the zenith point of your chart. If you want to get on it might be a good idea to mix business with pleasure whenever possible. However, don't chase attractive others because, if you do, you may discover that the boss is having an affair with them, and when you're found out this won't do your chances any good whatsoever, I think you'll agree.

Mars will be drifting along in the fiery sign of Libra, the area of your chart devoted to higher education and foreign journeys. If you're trying to better yourself, you will have to put in a great deal of effort but, believe you me, it will pay off in the long run. For heaven's sake, keep at it. If you happen to have a Libran in your life, you'll need to tread carefully at this time. They're going to be extremely tetchy and very short-tempered, and we don't want an explosion now, do we? Of course we don't.

1 FRIDAY Where people are concerned be prepared for the unexpected, their ideas will be genuine and original, and certainly worth considering, so don't let false pride stand in the way. It's likely, too, on a more personal level, that you could develop quite a crush on somebody. If this should be the case, it might be a good idea to try to discover in subtle ways how they feel about you.

≈

2 SATURDAY Cast your mind back to last year and recall the growth and adventures you experienced. Well, the planets are very similarly placed on this day, so that will give you a clue as to what to expect in the future. Strangely enough, the best qualities to complement this planet are hard work and practicality – which, of course, you have in abundance. Whatever happens, you mustn't let wonderful opportunities slip away because you're too slow to grasp them.

3 SUNDAY This is a time for discovering exactly who is going to back you, as well as who may free you from a rather unpleasant situation, because this could be the key to a successful future. You certainly won't rely on any kind of confrontation – in fact, perhaps a strategic withdrawal will be the way to progress at a slightly later date. Allow yourself plenty of time to assess the lay of the land; you'll be doing yourself a favour. A close relationship will do much to boost your confidence.

4 MONDAY Today is the day of the new Moon. It occurs in the watery sign of Scorpio, the area of your chart devoted to work and prestige. Certainly you seem to be doing well for yourself. It looks as if you're being applauded for past efforts, and that your boss will be watching. No crawling, though – you don't need to – your boss is already on your side.

5 TUESDAY You're certainly going to be doing very well for yourself if you're involved in a professional partnership or anything creative. Romance, too, can be found in connection with your job, although if you're already married you'll need to fight temptation if you want to stay that way. It won't do any harm to socialize with colleagues, just as long as you take your special person along with you.

6 WEDNESDAY The influence of a good friend is just what you need to take the edge off a rather tense close relationship. Don't allow yourself to get drawn into tense discussions, opt for a lighter and more relaxed social scene. While the planets have been livening up your professional matters, they may also have brought about some awkward moments. Getting away from it all is certainly more attractive than burning your fingers.

7 THURSDAY You're much more easily affected by what people think and do because the planets are highly sensitive for you right now. It's likely that you will appear to be more adaptable and changeable than you really are, and this new-found attitude is greeted with delight from those closest to you. Don't be surprised, though, if other people behave in a most extraordinary fashion.

8 FRIDAY The stars increase the artistic side of your nature, so you can produce some of your best work. If your career allows you to express your creative talents, then you can win the admiration you deserve. Equally, if you want to get into something that lets you achieve radical success, then just wait a couple of days. Those things nearest and dearest to your heart, whether people or activities, gain greater significance for the next couple of weeks.

9 SATURDAY There'll be times when you will feel less than certain of what you want out of life today. This is no bad thing, because you will at least seem to be more adaptable. On occasions when the ground seems to be slipping away from beneath you, turn to those you trust because they will be there for you. Entertain at home this evening with friends who make you laugh.

≈

10 SUNDAY There seems to be a suggestion of a new beginning in connection with professional matters. It's certainly a
great time for presenting your ideas, keeping a high profile
and generally being more dynamic. You do it, Aquarius, if
you want to. Now is the time to show the rest of us what you
can do, in no uncertain fashion.

11 MONDAY The stars could bring financial gain through
creativity and also intuition, so it might be a good idea to
listen to your inner voice instead of always using your practical, down-to-earth head. This evening, go to places you've
never visited before, perhaps with new people. You'll find this
very stimulating.

12 TUESDAY Paperwork and travel could be closely connected with your job. You're adaptable to what is going on
around you, and this new-found flexibility will greatly be
admired by your colleagues. Mix business with pleasure
whenever you see fit.

13 WEDNESDAY This is an important day, and one during
which you will be trying to decide which direction you
should be taking. On the one side you're full of new ideas; on
the other, there is doubt. Take courage from the optimistic
planets who are lording it up in your chart. Follow your
instincts, too, and have the courage to do what is necessary.
Your relationships will benefit from a dose of the truth.

14 THURSDAY Take advantage of prevailing circumstances
which crop up completely out of the blue. On the work front
you're highly stimulated, and even though you have more
than your fair share of work to tackle, you've loads of energy

≈

at your disposal. Don't be afraid to go after what you want and present your ideas. Should you believe a mistake has been made, speak up.

15 FRIDAY You could well gain from a stroke of luck; certainly you can take calculated risks, because they will pay off. If you're going to back a horse simply because its name has a special meaning for you, though, you could be out of pocket. So dredge up some common sense and you can make this day a profitable one.

16 SATURDAY Cash situations can certainly be improved, through past hard work that you took on and have now completed. If any chance to travel for the sake of your job crops up, don't hesitate because this will help you up another rung of the ladder of success. If you're socializing with colleagues this evening, don't be persuaded to spend more than you can realistically afford.

17 SUNDAY The planets are in an explosive mood. Because of this you may very well feel that you are moving in slow motion, while at other times you'll be working full throttle and charging through at an alarming rate. Remember, it's possible to act too quickly and impulsively and then live to regret it. This certainly seems to be the case with other people right now, so there's no need for you to feel the slightest envy.

18 MONDAY The common sense side of you is telling you to be content to plod along without taking any risks, but the opposite might be true in fits and starts throughout the day. Mind you, it only takes five minutes to make a 'botch up' of something, doesn't it, so slow down and make sure that you

≈

know all the possible difficulties of any job before you take it on, otherwise you'll finish up with egg on your face.

19 TUESDAY Try to keep a civil tongue in your head, because it won't take much to make you lose your formidable temper. This is probably because you're feeling a little unsure and insecure in yourself, so you really don't want to be bothered with difficulties and complications in other people's lives. Take care, my Aquarian friend, it'll be hard to get through the day without making at least one enemy.

20 WEDNESDAY Today is the day of the full Moon, and it is in the earthy sign of Taurus. Beware, this is not a day for tackling DIY or home improvements. Avoid calling a tradesperson in to do any work unless it is an emergency. You will only get ripped off. This is not a time for pushing your luck.

21 THURSDAY New faces and fresh places have no doubt helped to give you a different slant on life recently, but your real duties now seem to lie much closer to home. What's more, your integrity, honesty and talent for putting others at their ease will certainly be in demand; this is an excellent evening for inviting other people back to your home.

22 FRIDAY Today the Sun will be moving into the fiery sign of Sagittarius, the area of your chart devoted to friends, contacts and team effort – just the sort of thing you want to hear. You are the most friendly person in perhaps all of the zodiac, so the more you can mix with your fellows, the happier you will be.

≈

23 SATURDAY If you work as part of a team, you'll be able to put in more effort, which could result in some kind of breakthrough. Regardless of your profession, it's a time when others will be passing on useful tips and ready to give you the support you need to push into the wide blue yonder. Don't insist on plodding on regardless without help or advice from others.

24 SUNDAY It is true that on occasions you are frightened to express your feelings. Perhaps that's your lesson today, so let go, stop repressing the way you feel, and begin to think along more adventurous lines when it comes to the sexual side of life. Certainly you can be 'bawdy', but you can be adventurous too. Perhaps this is the day for finding out, so why not give it a try?

25 MONDAY It won't pay you to take long-standing social or romantic arrangements for granted. Get on the phone and double-check that everybody knows where they're supposed to be and at what time, because to be left hanging around for any length of time will turn you into a 'raging bull'. Remember, though, it's not their fault; the stars are stirring up everybody's grey cells, so make some allowances.

26 TUESDAY Today your social and romantic life seems to be running along smoother lines. You find it easier to take on any changes in your arrangements, and it's certainly a good time for lighthearted romance. Control the urge to leap in feet first, though, because although you may believe you've met the love of your life, perhaps the other person is only considering being your friend.

≈

27 WEDNESDAY Today you really can't rely on other people. For one reason or another they seem to be completely disorganized, perhaps through over-confidence. Certainly, socially they'll be a joy to spend time with, but you may find yourself tearing your hair out with frustration when you try to work alongside them. Try to be a little more open-minded – after all, we are all different.

28 THURSDAY Try not to overload yourself with too much responsibility, because this is a time when your resistance may be low, or you may tire far more easily than is usually the case. Perhaps you've been battling with problems for a considerable length of time and now feel that you must sit back and let others take over, which can be no bad thing.

29 FRIDAY If your ego has taken something of a bashing recently, and you're feeling a little inferior, or perhaps have allowed people to dictate what is or isn't going to happen, now is the time to put an end to all of this, because you won't receive any respect by going to extremes or playing the tyrant. You could be closer than ever to pressing your own self-destruct button, and that's because you've been suppressing your talents and personality for too long. Now is the time to take control of your life and let the stars lead you, but don't dare try to lead them. Be adaptable.

30 SATURDAY You're beginning a very sociable phase and one where the women in your circle may be important to you, not simply from a romantic viewpoint but for other reasons too, because they are handing on some good advice. Your ambition in life will seem to be a good deal clearer, and because of this you will feel more free to go after what you want. There's going to be a happy glow over club activities during the next couple of days, and you should visit your own particular favourite more often than you usually do.

DECEMBER

Until 21 December the Sun will be digging its way through the fiery sign of Sagittarius. Now, this is the area of your chart which rules team effort, friendship, casual acquaintances and, to a degree, your goals in life. There's quite a lot of activity on the social front at this time. Although you're very aware of the looming Christmas period, you're laughingly making efforts to save – but I shouldn't say that, I should encourage you.

On 22 December the Sun will be moving along into the sign of Capricorn, the area of your chart devoted to all that is hidden behind the scenes, your instincts and your imagination. If you are an artist of any description, be it a musician, painter, or even decorator, this is going to be a fortuitous time. Naturally, then, you'll be making things as beautiful as you can for the Christmas period, and any guests are going to be really lucky, they're going to be spoiled.

Mercury is also situated in Capricorn from 9 December onwards. Lots of minor changes in store, then. People born under the sign of Virgo or Gemini may be quite important at this time.

Venus will be drifting along in the water sign of Scorpio, the zenith point of your chart. This is good news because partnership affairs, particularly those that are professional, will be really thriving at this time and you'll be meeting a lot of new people and thoroughly enjoying yourself.

Mars is also in Scorpio all month, therefore, as the festive period is certainly approaching, this is a time when you'll be

≈

rushed off your feet, perhaps buying those last-minute presents which you'd probably forgotten – knowing you – well, you never really accept anything until the last minute, you can't be bothered to make plans, it just simply isn't in your blood.

The pattern made by the stars suggests that the majority of the planets are over the horizon, so regardless of what other people are doing you'll be making fresh starts in all areas, and seem to be rather excited and positive. Others may come to you for assistance or advice because they're drawn to your charisma, so give them some time. If you turn anyone away you'll feel lousy about yourself at the end of the year, and that would be a great pity.

1 SUNDAY Your self-confidence receives the kind of boost it needs to get you motivated. The next few days will give you so many exciting chances and opportunities that you can do no wrong in the favourable period that lies ahead. Don't turn down something on the basis that it went wrong before. This time you are perhaps wiser, and certainly more experienced, and should be able to measure up to the challenge.

2 MONDAY There's a lot of activity in the area of your chart which represents the intensely personal side of life. Don't put yourself first too much, because you may be seen as pompous. It might be a good idea to try to learn the lesson of humility. You're ready now to surf the oceans of life in search of new possibilities; soon the wave of success will sweep you up as the stars swoop down to help you fulfil an ambition. But, in all the excitement, don't slip back into your own stubborn and fixed ways.

≈

3 TUESDAY Today the stars indicate it's time to take some important professional decisions. If there's nothing special going on, why not sit down with loved ones and lay down a master plan so that you know exactly how to proceed in order to find greater fulfilment? For some of you there may be an unexpected opportunity to visit someone who lives at quite a distance. If so, it should be snapped up with glee and without trepidation.

4 WEDNESDAY You couldn't have a better time for chasing money which is owed you, although it will probably come trickling in all on its own. Be more adaptable and open-minded, too, as these are traits that those at work and at home are certainly going to appreciate. If you spend money today, you'll certainly be getting good value because, as usual, you're probably out looking for a bargain – you'll find one.

5 THURSDAY Every once in a while life throws up something which, at first glance, appears to be a little more than an irritating hurdle. The next few days will make it clear, however, that such things happen not merely to make life difficult, but to force you to make a painstaking review of your plans, hopes and dreams.

6 FRIDAY There's a strong possibility that you will feel like giving yourself a good kick. There's nothing wrong with you that a more positive outlook on life couldn't cure. So, instead of seeing the dark side of everything, try to look on the bright side of life for a change. If that doesn't work, get to the root of why you are so cautious and suspicious. Remember, you receive from others what you give out to them. Laugh and the world laughs with you; weep and, of course, you'll weep alone.

≈

7 SATURDAY The golden rule for you to remember today is not to resist whatever the stars have in store. This is the time for a dramatic reckoning in your life, when you must dispose of anything past its sell-by date. If you don't, the finger of fate will do it for you. Your future success is in the hands of others, and how well you do depends heavily on how you treat them on the way up.

8 SUNDAY You have several good reasons for trying to avoid tangles with family members over matters that could become explosive. In the long run, however, it may be wiser simply to allow these arguments to flare up as they will, and deal with the dramatics as you must, then put matters to rest once and for all.

9 MONDAY Today Mercury will be moving into the earthy sign of Capricorn, a rather secretive area of your chart. Minor changes are going on beneath the surface; it's up to you to stay alert and find out exactly what's going on. If you've a Virgo or a Gemini in your life, they could be of the utmost use to you. They've got plenty of good ideas for you to consider.

10 TUESDAY You seem to have been backed into a corner over matters which combine practical or financial affairs and your relations with loved ones, or projects about which you have passionate feelings. Whatever the exact situation, power struggles could easily waste your time and get you nowhere. While it may seem that standing your ground is the only way to deal with these issues, abandoning plans and thinking on your feet are likely to yield surprisingly worthwhile results.

≈

11 WEDNESDAY It's likely you may experience a couple of days when people with whom you work won't be as co-operative as they might be, so perhaps it would be a good idea for you to be prepared to plod on alone. In this way, not only can you achieve more but you'll also be freeing yourself from duties to others, which may have to be repaid in the future – something you might resent.

12 THURSDAY Progress in relationships may be difficult over the next couple of days or so. If you can persuade yourself that it is perhaps time for you to give without expecting any kind of reward, then the movement of the stars won't affect you in the least. If you are relying completely on other people to give you a helping hand, however, then you could be in for something of a shock.

13 FRIDAY You'll be meeting new people and will also be receiving some good news in connection with older friends. This is a good time for spending a couple of hours at a club, or perhaps involving yourself in some team sport, either as a participant or as a spectator. Either way, you'll certainly be sleeping soundly tonight.

14 SATURDAY The stars increase your intuition; the only question is, are you going to listen to it? I certainly hope so, because that is the only way to go forward during the next couple of days if you are to make the most of these opportunities which will be strewn in your path. Ferret around in the background of things, particularly if you have long-standing problems. Maybe you haven't done your homework properly. When you do, it becomes apparent what needs to be done.

≈

15 SUNDAY You're feeling much more confident about your ability to meet your commitments. Those of you who have been unsuccessfully chasing money should step up your efforts today, because it's a time when you can make your presence felt. Any kind of travel or paperwork can be lucky for you, so if you are expected to take this on, don't hesitate.

16 MONDAY The stars will throw you into the limelight, a place you normally avoid. But be a bit of a devil today, Aquarius, and make sure that others are aware of your needs and your wants. There's no point quietly sitting there hoping they can read your mind; there are times when you have to make the odd demand, and this is certainly one of them. So push ahead.

17 TUESDAY Stay in the centre of things and remember that most certainly your feelings are more easily moved at this time. Other people, who perhaps don't know you so well, frequently see you as a practical and detached individual, but now they will discover the softer side of your nature. But you needn't worry that they will take advantage. In actual fact, they are likely to be delighted to discover that you are human after all.

18 WEDNESDAY Try to play safe where personal and work matters are concerned. Certainly avoid all kinds of gossip, which you may be tempted to join in on, even adding a little embroidery. Concentrate instead on the personal side of life, which can be at its most fulfilling and enjoyable at this time. Cash problems seem to be fluctuating at the moment; they will settle down a little later on.

≈

19 THURSDAY Others, especially those at home, may be a bit difficult right now. Hopefully you can use your 'know-how' and stand aside a little when loved ones and children decide to spread their wings further than you would ideally prefer. This is also a time when cash matters need watching. On no account should you lend money or become involved in any kind of financial proposition. This would only lead to disappointment.

20 FRIDAY The stars will generate many new ideas, though it's unlikely you'll have a chance to put them into operation for a couple of days. In the mean time you can do some careful planning and fine-tuning so that, when the moment is right, you can step up to centre-stage and draw attention to yourself with your brilliance. Don't make it too much of a late night; you may run out of energy.

21 SATURDAY Superficially, at least, life seems to be relatively straightforward. Those closest to you will be at their most helpful and considerate. But remember that the stars are in a strange mood, and you may feel a little disenchanted as you suddenly become aware that there are still several obstacles to be cleared away. There could be some financial luck, however, perhaps through an artistic idea or project. This should cheer you up no end.

22 SUNDAY The stars today are opening up the minds of those closest to you; they are ready to give you any kind of support that you need – financial or otherwise. Be something of a little dare-devil then.

≈

23 MONDAY The stars emphasize property and changes in the family. There may be some exciting news of an engagement or a pending marriage, or even a birth, and you couldn't have a better couple of days for entertaining from home. You'll most certainly be making a big impression on your guests. You might have started Christmas a little early, but why not?

24 TUESDAY One pitfall you must watch out for today is not to go to extremes, because this could be unlucky for you. Nevertheless, there's a lively, colourful feel to today and this should put you in high spirits. You're ready for romance and, should the chance stroll pass, you'll be quick to grab it by the elbow.

25 WEDNESDAY Merry Christmas! The Moon will be coasting along in the earthy sign of Virgo today, the area of your chart devoted to team work. Hopefully everybody has been pitching in, because if they do, you'll all be getting a lot closer to one another. Try to stay away from family rivalries or 'spats', otherwise you'll spoil your time – and that would be a shame.

26 THURSDAY Today is a much more relaxed day, but even so your head is turning to the future. Perhaps you're getting a little bit stale, sitting around feeding your face. Well, it's a bit like that for all of us, isn't it? Why don't you sound out your mate, lay down those plans and get their approval?

27 FRIDAY In many ways you're quite glad the Christmas period is officially over, because now you are free to do exactly as you want, when and how, without considering others. By that, of course, I mean the family. Mind you,

≈

they've their own small fish to fry and you won't see too much of them until this evening, when you can exchange gossip.

28 SATURDAY It might be a good idea for you to rest up a little before the New Year celebrations get under way. It seems that you have been running around in circles over Christmas and your store of energy is all but depleted, so make this a 'please yourself' kind of day and don't allow other people to intimidate you or move you out of your home if that's where you want to be.

29 SUNDAY Everybody at home seems to be getting a little bit tired and irritable. Why don't you take them out into the fresh air and blow away the cobwebs? After all, there's New Year's Eve looming over the horizon, so it's too early to give up festivities just yet.

30 MONDAY There seem to be quarrels within two warring factions on the family front. Somebody's got to see some sense and, quite frankly, Aquarius, it might as well be you. Introduce some reality to the scene, because everybody has got everything out of proportion and you're just the person to sort it all out.

31 TUESDAY No doubt you've been inundated with chances to enjoy yourself. The only question has been, which to choose? Still, whatever you have decided to do, the ball is in your court and you're going to end this year feeling full of optimism for the year ahead. Mind you, 2002 shouldn't have been that unkind to you – in fact, in some ways it may have been quite spectacular. Happy New Year!

≋

Your Birth Chart
by Teri King

A Book of Life

Simply fill in your details on the form below for an interpretation of your birth chart compiled by TERI KING. Your birth chart will be supplied bound and personalized. Each chart costs £30.00 sterling – add £1.50 sterling for postage if you live outside the UK. Please make your cheque or postal order (cash is not accepted) payable to *Kingstar* and send together with your form to the following address: 6 Elm Grove Road, Barnes, London SW13 0BT, England.

Date of Birth _____ Time of Birth _____

Place of Birth _____

Country of Birth _____

Name _____

Address _____

_____

_____ Postcode _____

A birth chart also makes an ideal present! Why not include, on a separate sheet, the details of a friend or member of your family? Include £30.00 for each extra chart.